SAMSUNG
Galaxy S24
User Guide

The Ultimate Guide to Unlocking Features, Tips and Tricks for Seamless Integration and Maximum Performace

Randy Mellow

TABLE OF CONTENTS

INTRODUCTION

The Galaxy S24 Ultra, Galaxy S24+, and Galaxy S24 were introduced by Samsung Electronics, ushering in new eras of mobile experiences powered by Galaxy AI. Users' ability to be empowered by mobile devices will be eternally altered by the new age that the Galaxy S series ushers in. On the Galaxy S24 series, AI enhances nearly every experience, from setting a new standard for search that will change how Galaxy users discover the world around them to enabling barrier-free communication with intelligent text and call translations and maximizing creative freedom with Galaxy's ProVisual Engine.

Make Everyday Experiences Epic

With the introduction of meaningful intelligence, Galaxy AI aspires to improve every aspect of life, particularly the most essential function of a phone: communication. Thanks to the Galaxy S24, overcoming language hurdles is simpler than ever before. Have a conversation with a fellow international student or professional. While abroad on vacation, make a reservation. Live Translate, a two-way, real-time translation of phone conversations into text and speech, is what makes it all possible inside the native app. Our on-device AI ensures that all chats remain secret, and no third-party applications are needed. Using an Interpreter, two persons can have a live chat and simultaneously see a text transcription of the other person's words on a split-screen display. No Wi-Fi or cellular data is required for its operation. If you want your message to come out exactly as you meant it to, whether it's a kind note to a colleague or a brief and engaging statement for a social media caption, Chat Assist can help you refine your conversational tone in messaging and other applications. Moreover, the AIs included within the Samsung Keyboard can interpret texts in thirteen different languages in real-time. So you can remain connected without taking your eyes off the road, Android Auto will automatically summarize incoming messages and recommend appropriate answers and activities, such as telling someone your estimated time of arrival.

Note Assist in Samsung Notes is a great organizational tool since it includes AI-generated summaries, the ability to create templates that simplify notes using pre-made forms, and the ability to create covers that make notes simple to find with a quick preview. When recording audio with more than one speaker, Transcript Assist can employ artificial intelligence and speech-to-text technologies to do tasks like summarizing, translating, and transcribing. Beyond only improving communication, the Galaxy S24 series upgrades the phone's core features for the future. Looking anything up on the internet now affects almost every facet of our lives. As the first smartphone to introduce Google's intuitive, gesture-driven Circle to Search, the Galaxy S24 represents a watershed moment in the evolution of search. In a partnership with Google, the undisputed leader in search, Galaxy has provided its customers with an amazing new tool that enables them to discover new things with only a gesture. You can get useful, high-quality search results by circling, highlighting, scribbling, or tapping anything on the Galaxy S24 screen with a long hold on the home button. Without leaving the app, you can do an accurate search to discover more about a stunning location that appears in the background of a friend's social media post or an unexpected humorous fact on YouTube Shorts. For certain queries, users can acquire useful information and context from around the web via generative AI-powered overviews; they can also ask more complicated and nuanced inquiries. A child can do it. And the great one.

Samsung Galaxy S24 series: Design and specs

The two smaller phones, including the bigger phablet, have the same design language from Samsung, as is customary. Although it has a flat-screen and uses titanium all over its body, the Galaxy S24 Ultra otherwise appears very comparable to its predecessor. The first has been on S Pen devotees' wish lists for a long time, while the second gives the chassis materials a matte finish instead of the glossy metal that the Galaxy S23 Ultra had, which was a major improvement since it kept the screen cleaner.

Alternatively, you may be more acquainted with the Galaxy S24 and S24+. Thanks to lower bezels surrounding the display, the physical body of these two handsets is essentially similar to last year's phones, despite the somewhat bigger screens (6.2 and 6.7 inches, respectively). All three phones now support dynamic refresh rates ranging from 1-120Hz and have displays that are 2,600 nits brighter than the Ultra's panel. The Galaxy S24+'s upgrade to QHD+ resolution is icing on the cake.

Except for that, you probably already know what these gadgets are. You can't help but notice the iPhone-like flat edges on the two smaller phones the second you take them in your hand. The Ultra follows in the footsteps of Samsung's most recent smartphone models. Compared to its predecessor, it is somewhat slimmer at 8.6mm. There have been some little modifications to the design of the buttons, the bottom of the phone now has a speaker grill, and the top of the S Pen is flatter, but it still sticks out just enough to sway back and forth when you set it upright. Even if they are only rudimentary attempts to refresh the look, it's an improvement than Samsung doing nothing for the next generation.

Samsung Galaxy S24: Software

Launching with Galaxy AI, One UI 6.1, which is based on Android 14, draws a lot of attention. Still, the news of Samsung's revised software policy is the cherry on top. The Galaxy S24 series will continue to get software updates until 2031, much like Google's seven-year upgrade commitment, which was initially introduced with the Pixel 8. Not bad at all. The amount of artificial intelligence functions that are available on this phone is staggering, and to be honest, a little overwhelming. With Live Translate, you can have a phone conversation with someone while still using your original language. Several of Samsung's features seem to be an exact imitation of what's available on the Pixel at the moment. With Interpreter, Samsung takes a go at interpreting conversations and enabling split-screen communication.

A feature similar to Google's Magic Compose on the Pixel 8—Chat Assist—is included in the Samsung keyboard to assist with nail polishing. Aspiring journalists will find the S24 Ultra to be the ideal phone thanks to Transcript Assist, a Recorder clone, and Note Assist, an organizer for Samsung Notes' doodles and sketches. A new collaboration between Google and Samsung, this one for Circle to Search, was also announced. Launching on the Galaxy S24 and the Pixel 8 series, Circle to Search allows you to activate a shortcut from the navigation bar to quickly uncover extra context around anything you highlight on your phone. This seems to be a potent, but not exclusive, tool for anything from addresses to images. Artificial intelligence is certainly Samsung's focus this year, but whether or not all of these methods of interacting with your phone become standard issues is anyone's guess.

Samsung Galaxy S24: Cameras

The S24 Ultra continues the trend set by the Galaxy S23 Ultra with its massive 200MP main camera. After the S23 Ultra's disappointment with motion support, improved processing, optical image stabilization (OIS), and enhanced image stabilization (EIS), as well as bigger pixels on the main sensor, should result in greater low-light performance. Having said that, the telescopic lens undergoes the most significant alteration, which, at first glance, may not be an improvement.

The 50MP 5x optical zoom lens is an upgrade over last year's 10x 10MP lens, according to Samsung. You can still get 100x digital zoom, but we need to put these lenses through their paces to find out how the two generations stack up. The Galaxy S24 and S24+, on the other hand, have hardware that has remained mostly constant from one year to the next. However, once the phones are in our hands, we will be able to see the effects of improved processing on these lenses, which will significantly enhance their photo quality. No one was surprised to see AI in a film as well. The ability to eliminate reflections from window shots, along with features like Generative Edit and the new Instant Slow-mo function that uses artificial intelligence to slow down current recordings, is rather appealing, provided that they perform as advertised.

CHAPTER ONE
SPECIFICATIONS

Samsung Galaxy S24

With a sleeker design than the previous two years, cameras that can finally compete with the S24+, and a screen that is both brighter and adjustable to refresh rates ranging from 1 to 120 Hz, the smallest of Samsung's 2024 flagships has some of the series' most notable advances.

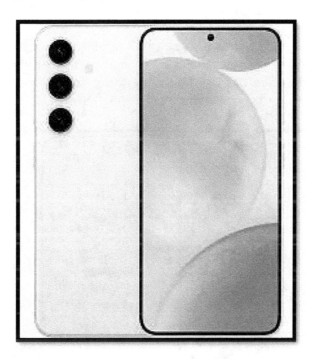

- **SoC:** Qualcomm Snapdragon 8 Gen 3 for Galaxy
- **RAM:** 8GB
- **Storage:** 128GB or 256GB
- **Battery:** 4,000mAh
- **Ports:** USB-C
- **Operating System:** Android 14 and One UI 6.1
- **Front camera:** 12MP, f/2.2
- **Rear camera:** 50MP, f/1.8 OIS main; 12MP, f/2.2 ultrawide; 10MP, f/2.4 telephoto (3× zoom)
- **Dimensions:** 147.1 x 70.6 x 7.6mm
- **Display type:** AMOLED, 1-120Hz
- **Weight:** 168g

- **Charge speed:** 25W wired, 15W wireless
- **IP Rating:** IP68
- **Stylus:** No
- **Display dimensions:** 6.2"
- **Charge options:** USB-C wired, Qi wireless
- **Cellular connectivity:** 4G LTE, 5G (sub-6 and mmWave)
- **Wi-Fi connectivity:** Wi-Fi 6E, Wi-Fi Direct
- **Bluetooth:** Bluetooth 5.3

Samsung Galaxy S24+

The Samsung Galaxy S24+ has an array of AI-powered capabilities, a brighter screen, and a stylish one-piece design. It delivers the same large screen and more functionality than the S24 Ultra but at a much more affordable price. One UI 6.1's ongoing improvements and seven years of upgrades let the software stand out on a phone with almost identical hardware.

- **SoC:** Qualcomm Snapdragon 8 Gen 3 for Galaxy
- **RAM:** 12GB
- **Storage:** 256GB or 512GB
- **Battery:** 4,900mAh
- **Ports:** USB-C
- **Operating System:** Android 14 and One UI 6.1

- **Front camera:** 12MP, f/2.2
- **Rear camera:** 50MP, f/1.8 OIS main; 12MP, f/2.2 ultrawide; 10MP, f/2.4 telephoto (3× zoom)
- **Connectivity:** NFC, UWB
- **Dimensions:** 158.5 × 76.2 × 7.6mm
- **Colors:** Onyx Black, Marble Gray, Cobalt Violet, Amber Yellow, Jade Green, Sapphire Blue, and Sandstone Orange
- **Display type:** AMOLED, 1-120Hz
- **Weight:** 197g
- **Charge speed:** 45W wired, 15W wireless
- **IP Rating:** IP68
- **Price:** $1,000
- **Display dimensions:** 6.7"
- **Display resolution:** 3120 × 1440
- **Charge options:** USB-C wired, Qi wireless
- **Cellular connectivity:** 4G LTE, 5G (sub-6 and mmWave)
- **Wi-Fi connectivity:** Wi-Fi 7, Wi-Fi Direct
- **Bluetooth:** Bluetooth 5.3

Samsung Galaxy S24 Ultra

The Galaxy S24 Ultra isn't a radical redesign, but it does have some notable differences from its forerunners, like a return to a flat display and seven years of software upgrades. This AI fad also works its magic on the Ultra's cameras for post-processing super slow-motion, and it's all centered on Galaxy AI and Google's newest services, including Circle to Search.

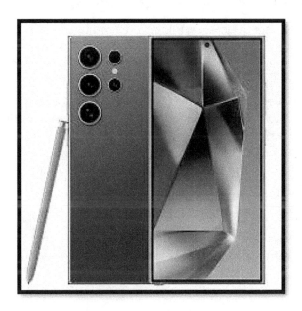

- **SoC:** Qualcomm Snapdragon 8 Gen 3 for Galaxy
- **RAM:** 12GB
- **Storage:** 256GB, 512GB, or 1TB
- **Battery:** 5,000mAh
- **Ports:** USB-C
- **Operating System:** Android 14 with OneUI 6.1
- **Front camera:** 12MP, f/2.2
- **Rear camera:** 200MP, f/1.7 main; 12MP, f/2.2 ultrawide; 10MP telephoto (3x); 50MP, f/3.4 telephoto (5x)
- **Connectivity:** UWB, NFC
- **Dimensions:** 162.6 × 79.0 × 8.6mm
- **Colors:** Titanium Black, Titanium Gray, Titanium Violet, Titanium Yellow
- **Display type:** LTPO AMOLED, 1-120Hz
- **Weight:** 233g
- **Charge speed:** 45W wired, 15W wireless
- **IP Rating:** IP68
- **Stylus:** S Pen included
- **Display dimensions:** 6.8", 19.3:9
- **Display resolution:** 3088 × 1440
- **Charge options:** Wired, wireless, reverse charging
- **Cellular connectivity:** 5G mmWave & sub-6, LTE
- **Wi-Fi connectivity: Wi-Fi 7**
- **Bluetooth:** Bluetooth 5.3

Features of the new Samsung Galaxy S24

If you think a smartphone cannot do everything, you need to check out the Samsung Galaxy S24 series. The Galaxy S24 series elevates your smartphone experience with innovative AI advancements. You can now search, communicate, and call in whole new ways that eliminate obstacles to productivity, language, and time. Invest in high-quality cameras that can shoot in low light and turn your social media accounts into picture albums. In addition, all of the devices in the line have strong CPUs, so you can play the best mobile games and multitask with ease. You can play and watch videos nonstop without worrying about running out of charge because of the large battery capacity.

Live AI Translation Tool

Amazing artificial intelligence makes the Galaxy S24 series function like a personal assistant that knows a lot of languages and is always up-to-date on the latest news. You can revolutionize your smartphone experience with the help of the Galaxy S24's highly powerful AI functions, which save you both time and effort.

You can anticipate the following from Galaxy AI and other Google features on the Galaxy S24:

- **Live Translate**: When you're overseas and need to dial a local number, you can use Live Translate. With Live Translate, you can communicate in your native tongue as the other person listens in theirs.
- **Note Assist**: Do you have little time? No sweat! With Note Assist, you can quickly and easily summarize any piece of written text into bullet points that anybody can scan and understand. You can also rearrange the paragraphs and titles, adjust the arrangement, and reformat.
- **Transcript Assist**: You can now delegate notetaking to Transcript Assist when you use it. Artificial intelligence records conversations, including who said what, so you may just listen or participate.
- **Chat Assist**: Whether you're composing a social media post or contacting a friend, Chat Assist can provide ideas in the perfect tone to help you express yourself more effectively.
- **Photo Assist**: Make your social media feeds look out with the aid of Photo Assist, an app that offers professional editing advice and applies stunning effects, such as blurring backgrounds or deleting unwanted objects or reflections.
- **Circle to Search with Google**: Whether you're looking for information on vacation places or the latest hairstyles, you can use Google's Circle to Search feature to discover what you need without touching the screen. Instantaneous search results are yours when you are just around the item.

Brightest & Sharpest Pictures

There is an excellent camera setup that is available throughout the Galaxy S24 smartphone series, and it is going to make your photographs seem more stunning than they ever have before. The Samsung Galaxy S series is well-known for having mobile camera setups that are at the bleeding edge of technology, and the most recent Galaxy S24 series does not fail in this regard. You can anticipate high-quality lenses that will turn your social media accounts into photographic masterpieces, and the upgraded artificial intelligence will take photographs that are tremendously brilliant and very sharp, even when it is dark outside. As an example, the new Galaxy S24 Ultra pushes the limits of what is possible concerning the photographic capabilities of smartphones. There is a remarkable 200-megapixel primary camera that captures everything your eyes perceive in a resolution that is as crisp as a pin and colors that are as gorgeous as nature. Thanks to the brand-new 50-megapixel telephoto lens, the revolutionary Quad-telephoto camera provides you with the ability to achieve optical zooms of 2x, 3x, 5x, and 10x. In addition, if you want even more, the astonishing 100x Space Zoom, which is driven by artificial intelligence, intelligently analyzes information to record photos and movies that are crisper and brighter from ludicrous distances, even when it is dark, thanks to the Nightography zoom feature.

Better Performance and Gaming Experience

There have been significant improvements made to the performance of the Galaxy S24 series, which means that everything you do on your phone will be elevated to a whole new level. Scrolling, streaming, and gaming can now be done for even longer periods thanks to the introduction of super-bright displays, strong CPUs, and long-lasting batteries. The Galaxy S24 Ultra indeed has the brightest screen ever seen on a Galaxy phone. It has a magnificent resolution of QHD+ and 2600 nits of brightness, which means that everything you view is of the highest possible quality. In addition, you can anticipate a gaming experience that is very lifelike as a result of the jaw-dropping visuals, which feature real-time shadows and reflections. In addition, the variable refresh rate comes in to give a gaming experience that is exceptionally smooth as the pace heats up. Not only are the hyper-responsive displays ideal for games, but they are also ideal for scrolling. They respond instantaneously to touch, providing you with outstanding control and engagement at all times.

About Android 14

More Customization

You could personalize your home screen for quite some time, but with Android 14, you'll have access to additional tools that allow you to customize your lock screen. A lock screen picker, certain lock screen templates, a monochrome theme, and support for Ultra HDR pictures are all included in this application. You can also build wallpapers with a parallax effect by utilizing your photographs, wallpapers with a cartoonish style that includes your preferred emoji, and even wallpapers with generative artificial intelligence that are based on text prompts.

Improved Battery Life

Even though no feature stands out, Google has made significant efforts to enhance the efficiency of Android to lower the amount of power that it consumes. As a result of modifications to the way the operating system handles background operations, downloads, and uploads, as well as a few other adjustments, Android users should be able to extract a little bit more life from their phone batteries. Additionally, it seems that the option to check "screen time since last full charge" in the battery settings menu, which was deleted in Android 12 and would now be available again, has been returned.

Notification Flashes

Within Android 14, you can activate camera flashes as well as screen flashes for notifications that are received. Although this feature has been accessible on other Android smartphones (such as Samsung devices) and iPhones for a considerable amount of time, it has not yet been integrated into the operating system itself. Alternately, you can switch on any one of them, or both of them and choose the color that will flash on your display. Its primary purpose is to assist those who have hearing loss; however, it can also be useful for anybody who does not want their phone to make a noise or buzz whenever a notification is received.

Better Hearing Aid Support

Hearing aids will no longer be grouped along with other Bluetooth devices, which is another piece of good news for those who have recently experienced hearing loss. You can choose which sounds should be sent to your hearing aids and which sounds should be transmitted via the device's speakers on a new page that is specifically devoted to hearing aids. Moreover, Android 14 will send you a pop-up message to alert you when you have been listening to loud music for an excessively long period. This is done to assist avoid hearing damage.

Better Support for Large Screens

During the first developer preview, Google announced that it would be assisting developers who were attempting to create applications that could adapt gracefully to varied screen sizes. When developers have access to a greater number of tools and design guidance, we can anticipate the development of applications that are compatible with tablets, folding phones, and smartphones. This would be similar to what Apple has done to ensure a smooth transition of its app ecosystem from the iPhone to the iPad to the MacBook.

Restricting Photo and Video Access

If you are uneasy about the all-or-nothing aspect of providing application access to your images and videos, you will be delighted to find that Android 14 has an option that allows you to choose which photos and videos the application is permitted to access. A comparable function was introduced by Apple in iOS 14.

Enhanced Security

Malware tends to target older versions of Android to circumvent the security changes that are included in later versions. As a result, Android 14 will not let you install older applications that were released before Android 5.1. There have been a few additional modifications made behind the scenes to enhance security, but possibly the most noticeable of these is the enhanced support for authentication using passkeys, which enables biometric login rather than the use of passwords for a greater number of applications.

Protected PIN

A Protected Personal Identification Number (PIN). Android 14 has yet another security and convenience boost for the modest PIN. If you want to make it more difficult for other people to steal your personal identification number (PIN), you can now disable the animations that play when you enter your PIN. It is also possible to remove the OK button at the end of your personal identification number (PIN) if it is six characters or more. Instead, you can have the PIN unlocked when you enter the last number.

Data Protection

The process of monitoring what applications and games are doing with your data is far more difficult than it ought to be. You could permit applications to access certain data depending on their policy when you install them, but what happens if they are purchased by another firm or alter their policy for some other reason and decide to sell your data to advertising or other third parties? A monthly notification will be sent to you by Android 14 if applications have altered their data-sharing practices.

Regional Preferences

Whether you want the temperature to be shown in Celsius or Fahrenheit, Monday or Sunday as the beginning of your week, or certain dates or numbers, you can define these preferences throughout the whole Android 14 operating system, and they will remain unchanged even after a backup or restoration operation has been performed. Additional enhancements include enhanced support for gendered languages such as French, as well as enhanced language adaptation depending on geographical location.

Predictive Back Gestures

To facilitate more intuitive gesture navigation, Google has included a large back arrow that is customized to match your background or theme. Coupled with predictive back gestures, which provide you with a peek of the screen that a swipe-back motion will take you to, it ought to be simpler for anyone to comprehend how to navigate and discover where they will end up. At the moment, it is not quite clear where a back swipe will take you with Android; it can take you to the home screen, it can take you to a previous screen, or it can take you to an application.

Health Connect

For example, you can use one app to monitor your smart scales, another app to monitor your jogging, and still another app to monitor your sleep. Although it is still in beta, the Google Health Connect app provides a means by which you can consolidate your data on your health and fitness and share it with other applications and services. All smartphones running Android 14 come with the application already installed, and it will automatically update itself.

Improved Share Options

Over a lengthy period, the share menu in Android has been inconsistent across a variety of Android devices and applications. Google has recently made it possible for applications to contribute their actions to system share sheets, and the ranking of your prospective share targets is now being determined by using additional data from applications. Because of this, you should be able to create a sharing menu that is more consistent and helpful, and that includes the applications and contacts that you want to share with.

CHAPTER TWO

SETTING UP YOUR DEVICE

Each of the three smartphones that make up Samsung's most recent flagship range is without a doubt one of the greatest smartphones currently available on the market. Whether you decide to get the Galaxy S24, Galaxy S24+, or Galaxy S24 Ultra, you can be certain that you will be able to get your hands on a fantastic smartphone that comes equipped with a flagship system-on-chip (SoC), a stunning display, outstanding cameras, and a great deal more. On the other hand, you will need to configure it before you can make the most of its hardware.

How to set up your new device

The process of setting up Samsung Galaxy devices is quite simple, and there are only a few small changes between it and the first setup experience on smartphones manufactured by other original equipment manufacturers (OEMs). You've arrived at the proper location if you're having trouble understanding a certain setting or if you're stuck at a certain level. This is a detailed guide that will walk you through the process of configuring your Galaxy S24 series smartphones.

1. To activate your Galaxy S24, click the power button until you see the screen shown in the image below. This will bring up the welcome screen.
- The power button is the side button on the right-hand side of the phone below the volume button.
2. From the drop-down menu, choose the language and area that you would like to use, and then press the Start button to begin the process of making the necessary configurations.

3. On the page that follows, choose the checkboxes that are located next to the End User License Agreement and Privacy Policy options, and then press the button that says "**Agree**." Select the checkbox that is located next to the option that says "**Sending of Diagnostic Data**" if you wish to provide diagnostic data to Samsung to assist the firm in enhancing the quality of its software experience. If you do not want to be sharing diagnostic data with Samsung, you should skip this step.

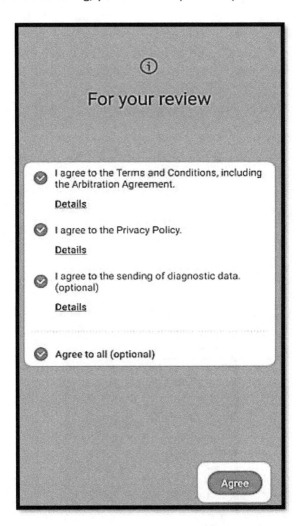

4. On the screen that follows, the setup wizard will inquire as to whether or not you would want to transfer settings, accounts, and other information from your previous device to your new Galaxy S24. If you are copying data from an Android device, choose the Galaxy or Android device option. If you are switching from an Apple device, use the iPhone or iPad option. Not interested in copying data and setting up your Galaxy S24 as if it were a brand-new phone? Find the button labeled **"Skip"** in the lower-left corner of the screen.

5. To connect your Galaxy S24 to the internet, please choose your Wi-Fi network from the list that appears on the next screen and then log in using your password. Your ability to successfully finish the parts of the setup procedure that call for an active internet connection will be facilitated by this. If you want to use a Google account to log into your device, you can skip this step; however, you should not do so.

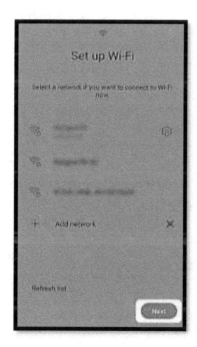

6. If you already own an eSIM, you can add an eSIM to your phone by using the QR code scanner on the following website to configure it after you have already purchased it. If you want to use a real SIM card, you can skip this step, since it is not required.

7. After you have finished setting up your eSIM, you will be presented with a screen where you can select to transfer all of your applications, photographs, contacts, and other Google Accounts from your previous device to the Galaxy S24. If you choose to transfer data from your previous device, select **Next** and then proceed to follow the instructions. If you want to set it up as a new device, you can skip this step by pressing the **Don't copy** option.

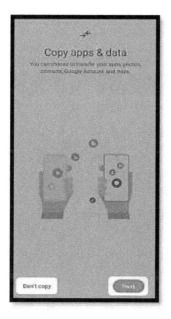

8. If you wish to utilize Google applications and services, such as the Play Store, Gmail, and other similar services, you will need to sign in using the credentials associated with your Google Account on the following screen. Immediately after the retrieval of your account information by the setup process, you will be required to consent to Google's terms and privacy policy. If you wish to back up your data and simply recover it when you transfer to a new device, you can then choose to activate or disable backups from Google Drive.

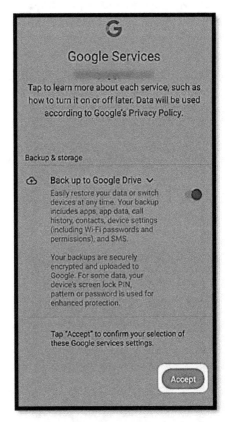

9. You will be prompted to set up a screen lock on your Galaxy S24 once you have completed the process of setting up your Google Account. Your fingerprint can be used for biometric authentication, you can add a new password, pattern, or personal identification number (PIN), or you can set up face unlock. For reasons of safety, you will be required to create a secure password or personal identification number (PIN) before adding a new fingerprint if you want to utilize the fingerprint option.

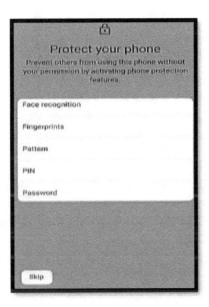

10. Once that is finished, you will need to activate or disable the Google Assistant hotword to access the virtual assistant with your voice. Additionally, you will need to set up lock screen access to the Google Assistant in the steps that follow.

11. After that, the setup wizard will ask you to sign in to your Samsung account for further instructions. If you do not set up your Samsung account, you will not be able to utilize some Samsung applications, such as Galaxy Store and Samsung Members, even though this step is completely optional.

12. After that, the wizard will ask you to choose and download the Samsung applications that are suggested to you on the page that follows. If you do not want to enable the installation of the applications on your device, you can skip this step.

13. After that, you will be given the option to either activate or disable certain Samsung services, such as the Continuity Service, the Customization Service, and the Nearby device scanning. Simply pressing the toggle that is located next to each option, you can either activate or disable these services.

14. On the screen that follows, choose whether you want to use the Light or Dark theme for the user interface, then decide if you want to proceed with the next step. When you choose **Finish**, your device will be completely configured and ready for use.

How to charge the battery

To charge the battery of your S24, follow these general steps:

1. **Use the Original Charger:**
- The first piece of advice is to always use the charger that comes with your phone. A USB Type-C cable that is both compatible and reversible will be included with your new device. Use a charger that is compatible with the s24 if you don't have the charger that came with the phone.
2. **Connect the Charger:**
- Insert the charging cable into your phone's charging port and the charger's USB port.

3. **Connect to Power Source:**
- Insert the charging cable into an electrical outlet or computer USB port. Confirm that the power source is turned on.

4. **Monitor Charging:**
- A charging symbol or indication should be visible on your phone's screen.

5. **Wait for Full Charge:**
- Let your phone charge till the battery level is adequate.
6. **Disconnect the Charger:**

When your phone is completely charged, remove the charger cord from both the device and the wall outlet. If you want your device to charge safely and efficiently, make sure you use a good cable and adapter. Additionally, stay away from using low-quality or fake chargers since they do not have enough safety features and can end up harming your phone's battery.

How to power on/off your device

If you need to turn your device on after it has been turned off, please follow the steps below.

Here are the steps to follow:

1. Hold the device firmly in your hand.
2. Then, to turn the device on, press and hold on the side button. Underneath the main volume button is the tiny button that serves as the side button.

3. To power down the device, just press and hold the side key and volume down buttons simultaneously.

4. In the menu that pops up, choose the **power-off** option.

How to transfer data from an old device to your new Galaxy S24

Pictures, videos, notes, contacts, calendars, music, and messages are just some of the many data that can be transferred from one smartphone to another using the **"Smart Switch"** feature. Keep in mind that Smart Switch requires a computer, Wi-Fi, or a USB connection to accomplish these transfers. Transferring data from an older device to a new Galaxy is a breeze using the included USB cable.

1. Link your mobile devices

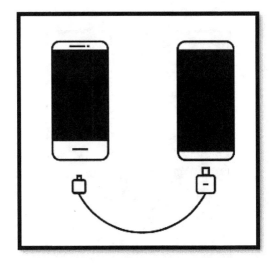

2. Slide up and choose Smart Switch.

3. Get the old device scanned.

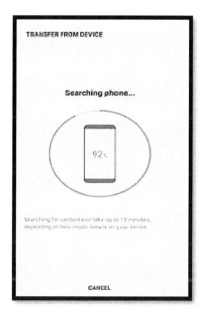

4. Pick out the exact files or information you want to send.

5. The functionality of the Smart Switch is complete. From your previous device to your new Samsung Galaxy S24, all of your selected contents will be seamlessly transferred.

How to use wireless power-sharing

With the new PowerShare function, available on Samsung's Galaxy smartphones and wearables, you can share your battery power with other devices that have the same capability. Your Galaxy device's battery life might be extended by connecting it to another device that supports PowerShare.

Using the PowerShare function to charge your device is as simple as following these steps:

1. From your home screen, locate and choose **Settings**.
2. Go to the **Battery and Device Care** section. Select **Battery**, followed by **Wireless Power Sharing**, after you are through.

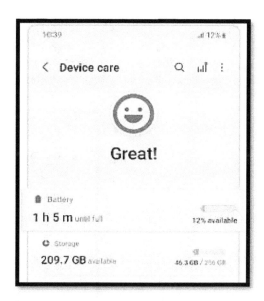

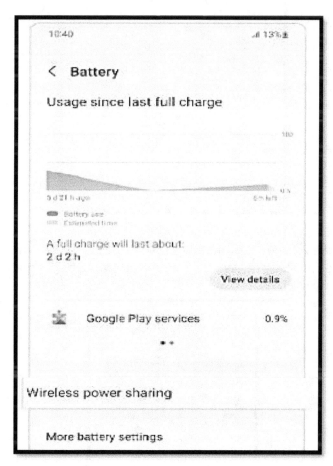

3. To enable the **wireless power-sharing feature**, tap ⊙.
4. After that, go to the **Battery limit option** and choose the percentage you want (**note:** if you choose a percentage, wireless power-sharing will be turned off automatically when the charge level of your device reaches that %).

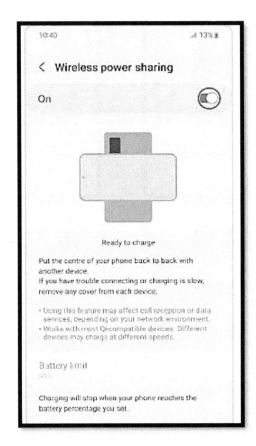

5. Hold your smartphone with the screen facing down. (**Note:** When you experience a vibration or a notification sound, it signals the device has begun charging.) Next, place the compatible device on top of it.

You can utilize the wireless power-sharing capability on most Qi-certified devices, but you need to charge them to at least 30% before you can transmit power.

The following considerations should be given serious thought while using the wireless power-sharing feature:

- Please note that some covers or accessories could impede the proper functioning of the wireless power-sharing function, thus it is important to remove them before utilizing the feature.
- The availability of Internet service or phone reception might be impacted by your network environment.
- The wireless charging coil can be repositioned on various devices, and the rate of charging can change based on the device's condition. Therefore, for the connection to take place, you'll need to change your location. To verify the link, just wait for a notification or vibration.

CHAPTER THREE
GETTING STARTED

How to insert SIM cards

Putting a SIM card into your S24 is as simple as:

1. Turn off the SAMSUNG Galaxy S24 before anything else.
2. The second step is to find the slot for your SIM card on the SAMSUNG Galaxy S24. It will be easy to spot because of the little hole that the eject tool fits into.
3. Push the SIM card tray out of its slot using a SIM removal tool. In the absence of a SIM removal tool, you can use a paperclip or a pushpin as an alternative.
4. SAMSUNG Galaxy S24 SIM card tray removal follows suite.
5. Place your SIM card in the slot. Return the SIM tray to the phone by pushing it in.
6. Activate the SAMSUNG Galaxy S24 and connect it to a mobile network.

How to customize your home screen

From matching the user interface to your wallpaper to installing themes that alter the entire appearance of the Home screen, Samsung offers a plethora of Home screen customization options to ensure that your Home screen serves your purposes, even if it may seem quite plain first upon setup.

The Samsung Galaxy S24's home screen can be customized in the following ways:

1. Go to the home screen of your Galaxy S24. Press and hold anywhere on that home screen. The picture below shows the menu that displays after that action.

2. To personalize your background, you will need to tap on **Wallpaper and style**. Touch **Wallpaper and Style** in the bottom-left corner of the Home screen customization menu.

Then, touch **Change wallpapers** to change the wallpaper for both the Home screen and the lock screen.

If you want to customize the color palette of your user interface to go with your wallpaper, you can do so by tapping **Color Palette** from this menu. You can choose one of several options that are compatible with your current wallpaper, or you can make your own unique choice. Simply hit the Apply button to commit your changes.

3. Select a theme for your Home screen by tapping the **Theme** option. Your closest friend in the home screen customization department will be themes if you're looking to do more than just alter the background. This isn't a novel idea for Android; in fact, it's been around for quite some time. However, it will alter not only your wallpaper but also the color scheme and icons used in the user interface.

You can access Samsung's dedicated Theme shop from the Home screen customization menu when you choose **Theme**. Download, and install any theme you prefer by pressing that Theme at the bottom.

4. On that Home screen, tap on **Widgets** to add a new one.

Customize navigation gestures

Instead of the more natural gestures for navigating, Samsung phones come with navigation keys. After you've finished setting up your Samsung phone, like the Galaxy S24 Ultra, the first thing you should do is switch to gesture navigation.

1. Launch Samsung's **Settings** app on your phone.
2. Select **Display**.
3. Scroll down till you get to the **Navigation bar**. Select it
4. To switch to navigation gestures, tap the **Swipe gestures**.
5. You can adjust the sensitivity of the gesture and toggle the assistant app gesture on and off in the **More options** menu.

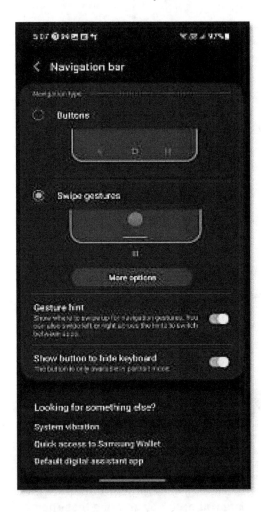 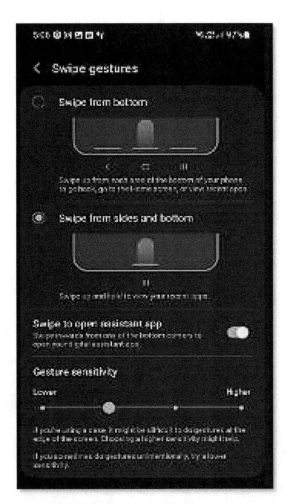

6. However, there is another, less obvious **Swipe from bottom** gesture that you can use.

How to manage your notification

Here are the steps to manage your notification:

1. Begin by sliding down at the top of the screen.

2. Go to the settings menu by tapping the gear symbol 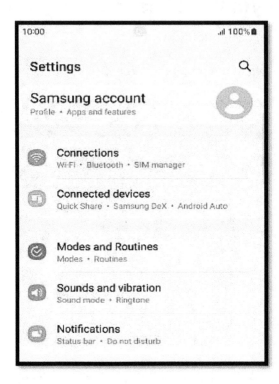 in the upper right corner.
3. Press **Notifications**

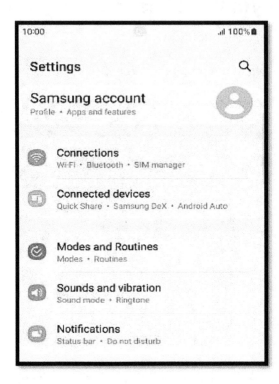

4. Tap on **App Notifications**

5. Next to the "All" option is the down arrow▾ . Press it

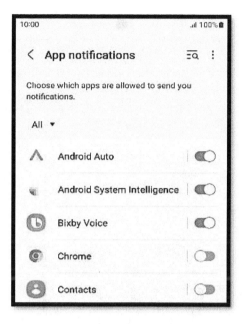

6. Go to the settings menu and pick which applications you would want to get notifications from.

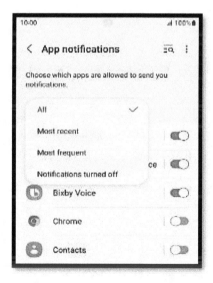

7. To activate or deactivate the feature, press the corresponding indicators next to each program.
8. To get back to the main/home screen, press the home button ▢ .

How to lock and unlock your device

Like any other modern device, yours includes a lock feature that can be used to safeguard it and stop unauthorized users from accessing it.

How to lock and unlock your device using the side keys according to the settings:

1. To lock your smartphone, press the side button that's adjacent to the volume controls on the device.

2. However, if your smartphone is locked and you hit the key located on its side, your device will be unlocked.

How to add a Google, Samsung, and Outlook account

The many accounts you will wish to add may support calendars, email, contacts, and a plethora of other features—all under your control—on your brand-new Galaxy S24.

How to add a Google account

With a Google account, you can install apps directly onto your device and have access to Google Cloud Storage.

The process is as follows:

1. Select the **Settings** app from your Home Screen.
2. Afterwards, choose the **Accounts and Backup** option.
3. The third option is to choose **Manage Accounts**.
4. Select the option to **Add Account**, and then provide the account that will be added (Google)

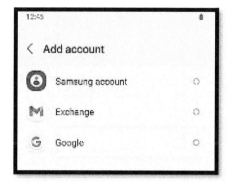

Please be informed that when you log in to your Google account, Factory Reset Protection will be enabled. This information is crucial. Your Google account information will also be required should you choose to reset your device to factory settings.

How to add a Samsung account

With a Samsung account, you can enjoy Samsung-exclusive content and use a wide range of Samsung apps. **Here is the procedure:**

1. Launch the **Settings app** by selecting it from the Home screen.
2. Discover the **Samsung account** option and choose it.

How to add an Outlook account

To see and manage your incoming email messages, you will need to connect an Outlook account. **Here is the procedure:**

1. Locate the **Accounts and backup** option on the Settings app.
2. Pick the **Manage accounts** option.
3. Additionally, go to the Add account option and choose Outlook as the kind of account you want to add.

How to set up voicemail

Depending on your carrier, you can have several options when it comes to accessing your voicemail on your smartphone, however, you can use the Phone app. **Here is the procedure:**

1. From the Home Screen, touch the Phone app's icon to launch it.
2. The second step is to press and hold the 1 key. One other option is to click the "Voicemail" button.

3. Make a password, enter your location, and enter your name according to the directions that appear on the screen.

How to restart your device

Following these steps will restart your s24 device:

1. **Hold the power button and the volume down button simultaneously.**

Hold down the volume down and power keys on the right side of the Galaxy S24 simultaneously. Hold on tight until the second step's menu displays.

2. **Choose Restart.**

A menu with options to turn off the phone, restart it, or make an emergency call should show after three seconds of tapping and holding the power and volume down keys. Select **Restart** from the menu.

3. To confirm, tap **Restart** once again.

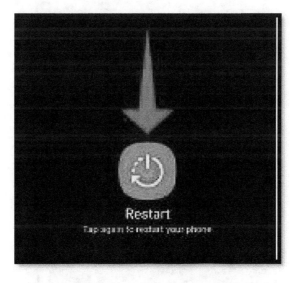

With the removal of everything except the Restart button will be shown. To restart your Galaxy S24, press and hold the button again. If not, you can exit by tapping anywhere else on the screen.

CHAPTER FOUR

HOW TO DISABLE THE APP DRAWER

Not a fan of the app drawer? You can hide it if you like, and then use several home screen pages to showcase all of your applications and games. Here's how:

1. On the home screen of your Galaxy phone, long press a space.
2. Choose **Settings** from the bottom-most option that appears.

3. Select the **Home screen layout**.

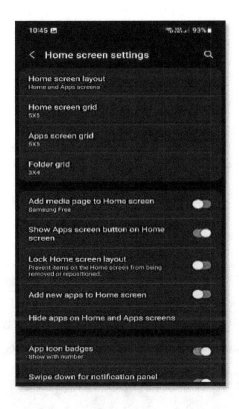

4. Choose **Home screen only**.
5. To make the changes official, tap **Apply**.

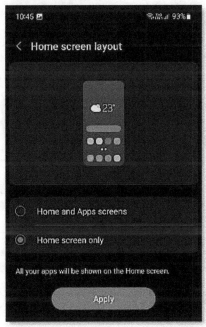

Return to the main screen of your phone. On several home screen pages to the right, you can see the installed applications. You can access system settings, applications, files, and more using the Finder search by swiping up on the home screen while the app drawer is disabled.

How to hide unwanted applications

On your Galaxy phone, is it possible to hide some applications from the home screen and app drawer? From the One UI settings menu, you can do so. With all the bloatware and applications that come preloaded on Galaxy S24 and other premium phones, this is a great option.

1. Go to your Galaxy phone's **settings** app.
2. Find the **Home screen** menu by scrolling down.
3. Choose the **Hide apps on Home and Apps screens** option.

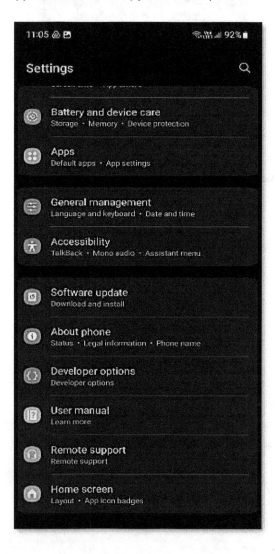

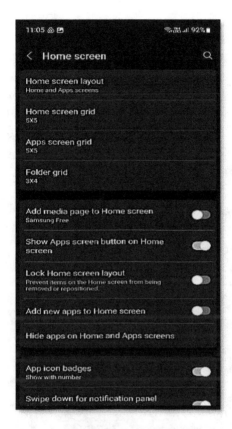

4. To hide certain applications, choose them.

5. In the Hidden applications area, your chosen apps will be shown at the top.

6. To save the changes, tap the **"Done"** button at the bottom.

How to stack widgets

You can create a stack of widgets using Samsung's One UI launcher. In this manner, your main home screen can accommodate several widgets without seeming cluttered. Learn how to arrange widgets on the home screen of your Galaxy phone in this guide.

1. Press and hold an empty spot on the home screen for a few seconds.
2. The second step is to go to the bottom menu and choose **Widgets**.
3. Choose a widget to add to your home screen and move it to the desired location. The widget can also be added to the home screen by tapping the "Add" button.

4. After adding a widget to your home screen, long press on it.
5. Pick the option to **Create Stack**. An inventory of the widgets that can be stacked upon the first widget is shown.

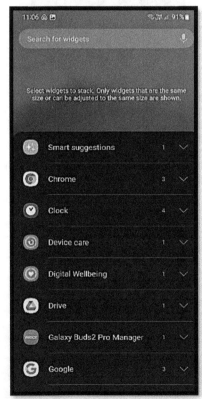

6. Once you find one that suits your taste, just touch the Add option.

You can swipe through the widgets in a stack by swiping left or right.

How to change the grid size on the home screen

You can change the grid size of the home screen and app drawer on Samsung. To create extra room for widgets and app shortcuts, you may want to adjust the grid size layout on your Galaxy phone if the default home screen layout is too small.

1. On the home screen of your Galaxy phone, long press on a space.
2. Choose **Settings** from the bottom-most option that appears.
3. Press the **Home screen grid**.

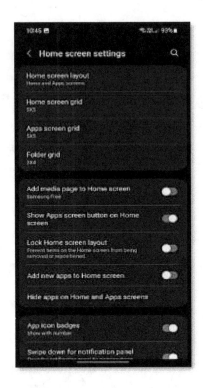

4. Select the preferred grid arrangement.
5. To adjust the size of the grid in the app drawer, tap the Apps screen grid option.
6. Pick a size for the **Folder grid** between 3x4 and 4x4.

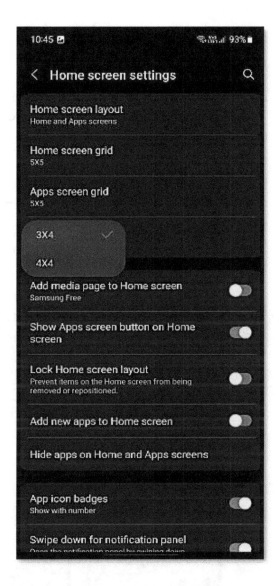

How to max out the screen resolution

S24 devices like to be set at FHD+, which is 2316 x 1080 when you are setting them up. Even though it's not the most your device can handle, 1080p HD material looks good enough to pass. Leaving it there will severely restrict your experience, particularly when using 1440p streaming applications.

1. Launch the **settings** app on your Galaxy S24.
2. When you see **Display**, tap on it.
3. Tap on **Screen resolution** after scrolling.
4. Pick **WQHD+.**

52

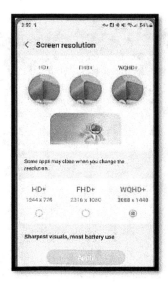

Be aware that the Galaxy S24's battery life can be negatively affected if you choose the maximum resolution, which can reduce your daily battery life estimate. As far as I can tell, even with the maximum resolution set, the S24 Ultra is more than enough to last a whole day. If you notice a decrease in speed, you can easily restore 1080p as the resolution. Alternatively, you can choose 720p to maximize the 5,000mAh battery's potential and get even more use out of it.

How to enable or disable the edge panel

1. Find the Settings icon ⚙ in the Notification bar and swipe down to access it. Find **"Display"** and select it.

2. To activate or deactivate the Edge panels, find and click on the corresponding switch.

Access and use the Edge Screen

1. Choose the Edge panel's handle and move it to the left.

2. The second step is to choose an option.

Access and edit Edge panel settings

1. Pick Edge panels and then Panels from the screen where you can see the display.

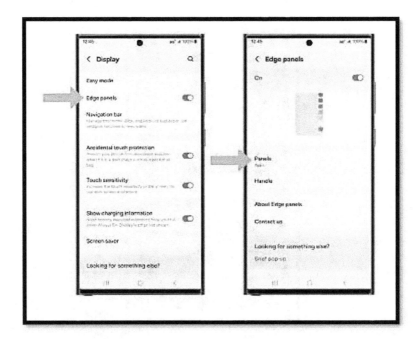

2. Change the settings to your liking

- **ADD/REMOVE A PANEL:** Click the circle that appears over the panel you want to edit.
- **EDIT APPEARANCE:** To change the look of a panel, click Edit located underneath it.

CHAPTER FIVE

ABOUT BIXBY

The great majority of Samsung users should already be familiar with Bixby due to its widespread use. One feature, Bixby, has the potential to function as an intelligent virtual assistant that can comprehend, learn from, modify, and adapt to your preferences. After it gets to know your routine on a daily or monthly basis, it can help you set up reminders at the best times and in the most convenient places.

To activate Bixby on your mobile device, follow these steps:

1. Press and hold the **Side button** for a few seconds after unlocking your smartphone and going to the Home screen (**NB:** Bixby can also be triggered from the Apps list).

How to use Bixby Routines

Using their present location and the activities they are performing, owners of the Samsung Galaxy S24 series can use Bixby to show information or change the settings of their smartphones. **Here is how to utilize it:**

1. Launch the **Settings app** from your device's Home screen.
2. Pick the **Routines tab** in the **Modes and Routines** section of the **Settings** menu.

Add a routine

1. To add a trigger to the routine, click the Add icon under **routine**. Then, under **If**, click the Add icon.

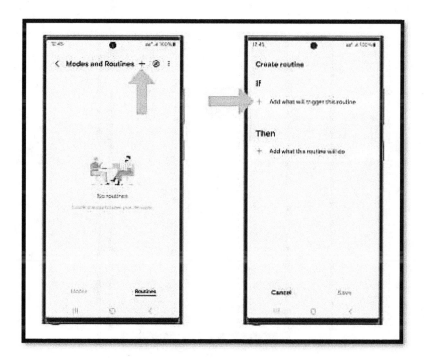

2. Choose the trigger you want. Pick **Done** after making any necessary changes to the settings.

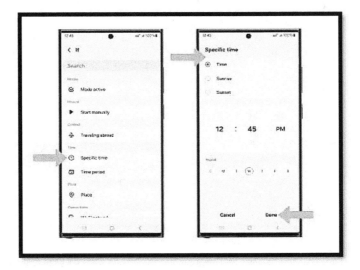

3. To specify the action that the routine will do, click the Add icon located beneath the Then section.

Note: You can add more triggers by following the on-screen instructions once you click the "Add condition" button⊕ in the "If" section. Pick the Remove symbol⊖ to get rid of a trigger.

4. Pick the thing you want to do. Make any necessary changes to the settings and then click the **"Done"** button.

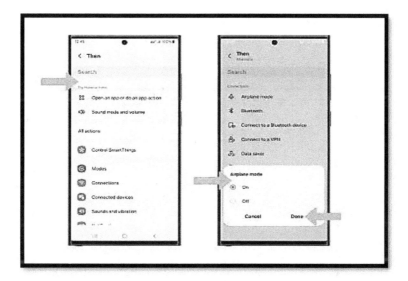

5. Click **"Save"** when you're through. Name the Routine you want to create, and then hit the **"Done"** button.

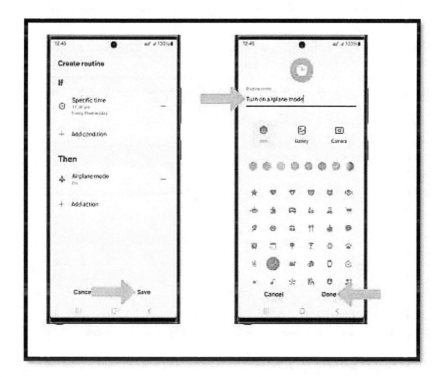

Disable or enable a routine

1. A routine is automatically activated upon creation. Pick the routine you want to deactivate. To disable this process, click the "More" button⋮.

Note: The confirmation will be shown, and you will need to click **Disable this routine** to proceed.

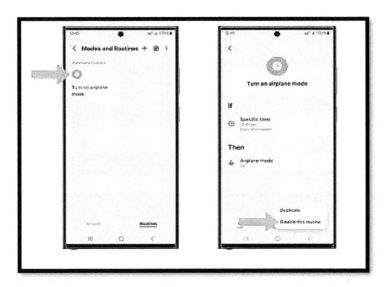

2. Pick the deactivated routine you want to restore, re-enable, and hit the **Enable** button.

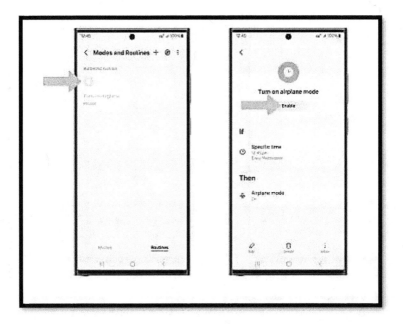

Delete a routine

Press and hold the routine(s) you want to remove, and then choose the **Delete** icon.

Note: Another confirmation question will appear, asking you to choose Delete again.

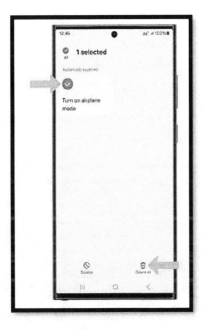

Access Bixby Routine settings

After you've clicked the menu icon ⋮, go to Settings. Go ahead and change the settings as you want.

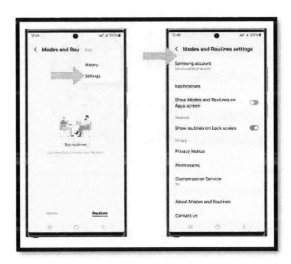

How to use Bixby Vision

With this feature, you can make better sense of what you're seeing in the Gallery, Internet, and Camera apps on your device. Along with this, it gives you contextual icons that can translate content, scan QR codes, and e-commerce.

What follows is a rundown of the Camera's Bixby vision features:

1. Pick up the Camera app from the main menu.
2. To access **BIXBY VISION**, swipe left to **MORE** and then tap on it.

An informational screen outlining the terms and conditions and privacy notice will appear if this is your initial visit to Bixby vision. Click on Continue.

3. After that, choose DISCOVER and then aim the camera of your device at something or somewhere. Bixby Vision will automatically recognize the item or place.

4. Choose the desired search output.

Access Bixby Vision settings

Navigate to select Settings by clicking the **More Option** ⋮ on the Vision screen. Tailor the parameters to your liking.

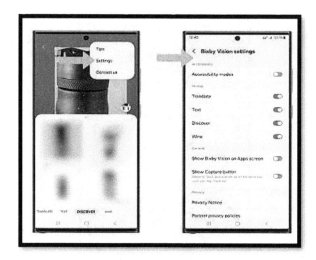

Parental Controls and Digital Wellbeing

By checking the digital wellbeing and parental controls every day, you can see how often you use apps, how many notifications you get, and how often you glance at your device, giving you the ability to monitor and restrict the use of your smartphone.

How to make use of these functionalities is explained below:

1. To access the following functionalities, launch the **Settings** app and go to **Digital wellbeing and parental controls.**

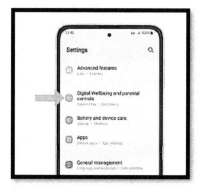

- **Number of daily notifications:** The amount of alerts you get from each app each day: Be careful to keep track of this metric.
- **Unlock:** You get the ability to see the daily application startup counts.
- **Screen time:** Check the statistics for screen time to see how long an app has been accessed and utilized daily.

Several ways to disconnect

- Change the grayscale, mite alarm, and call volume at a predetermined hour using the **Bedtime mode.**
- If you're trying to get some work done and want to keep distractions to a minimum, you may want to try switching to **Focus mode**.

Your goals

- **App timers:** Choose how long you'd want to spend each day on your preferred app and set a daily limit for yourself.
- **Screen time:** Set a daily goal for the amount of time you want to spend in front of screens and track your progress against that goal.

Check on your children

- Google Family Link has parental controls that let you keep tabs on your kids' device use. This feature allows you to choose the apps your children use, set screen time limits, and filter the material they can access.

Comfort care

- **Monitor volume:** Select a sound to serve as a volume monitor, protecting your eyes from potential harm.

Enable or disable Focus mode

1. To access the modes and routines, go to the settings panel and either choose an option or click the plus sign.

2. To begin, choose **Start**. To activate the focus mode, choose the appropriate situation, and then modify the parameters according to your liking by following the on-screen instructions. Click **Next** when you're done.

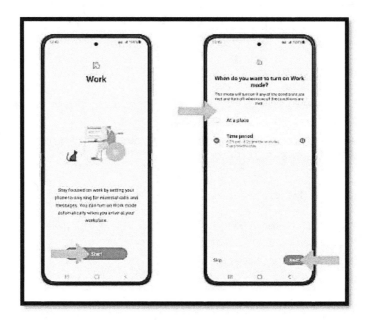

3. Choose **Next** after making any necessary changes to the Do not disturb settings. When your phone is in "Do not disturb" mode, you won't get any incoming calls or app alerts. Choose "App notifications" to enable push alerts from certain applications. Select the Add apps icon. Select apps as desired, then select **Done**.

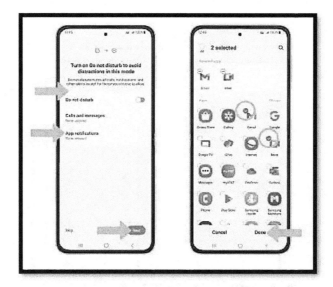

4. Just make the changes you want and hit the **"Done"** button.

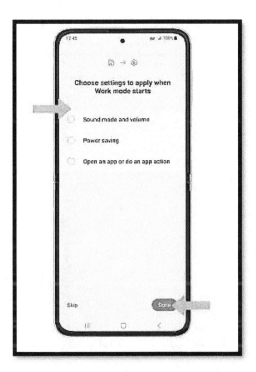

5. Choose Turn on to activate Focus mode manually. Choose Turn off to turn off Focus mode.

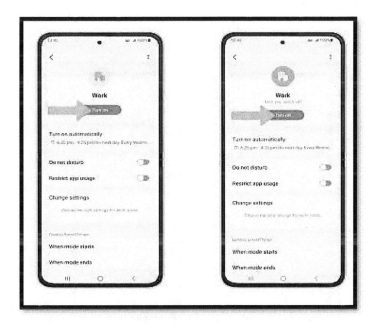

Set app time limits

1. Find the App timers option in the Digital Wellbeing & parental settings menu.

2. To modify the timer, choose the program you want to use it with and click on its icon. At the end, click the **"Done"** button.

Note: Some system applications do not have timers.

3. Pick the timer symbol beside the app you want to remove it from, and then tap the **discard** option.

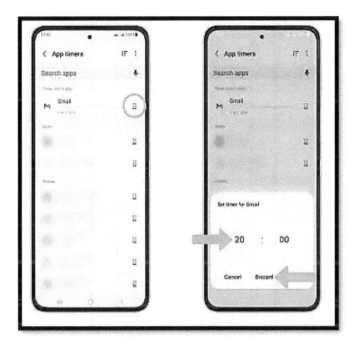

Enable or disable Bedtime mode

1. Choose **Sleep** from the **Modes and Routines** menu, and then hit **Start**.

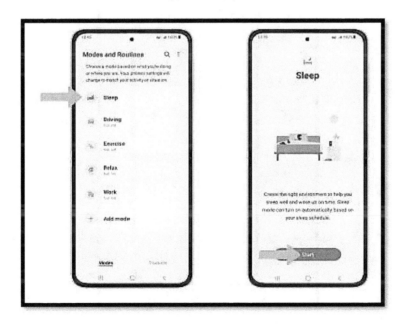

2. Click **Next** once you've made your selections for the ideal sleeping and waking times.

3. Choose **Next** after making any necessary changes to the Do not disturb settings.

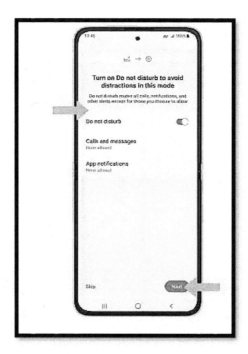

4. Once you've made any changes to the Sleep mode settings, click **Done**.

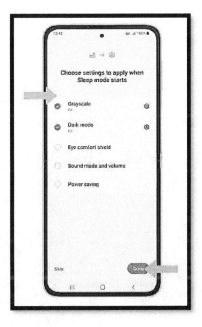

5. Choose **Turn on** to activate Sleep mode manually. Choose **Turn off** to turn off Sleep mode.

How to use the Always-on Display feature

Thanks to a feature called Always On Display, users can see the date and time, missed call alerts, missed message notifications, and more without unlocking their smartphone.

This function can be used in the following way:

1. Pick **"Lock screen"** after opening the **Settings** app.
2. Press the **"Always On Display"** option.

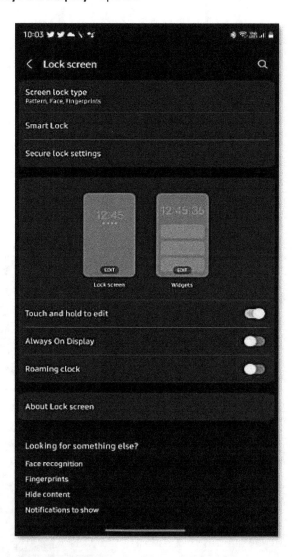

3. To activate it, tap the button on the top right side of the screen; then, choose the mode that works best for you.

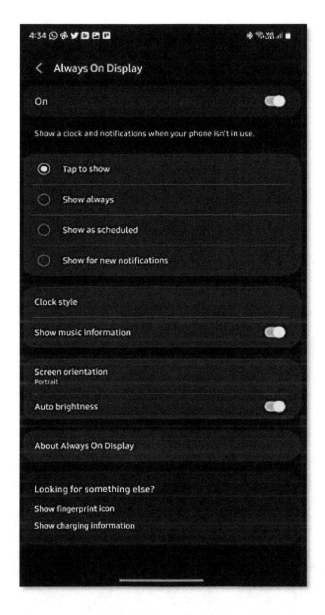

- **Tap to show:** When you touch the screen, the Always On Display will be visible for a brief moment.
- **Show always:** When the phone is locked, the Always On Display will be visible at all times.
- **Show as scheduled:** You have the option to decide in advance when Always On Display will be seen. You can set it to just show up during the day and turn it off at night, for instance.
4. The Always On Display's clock can be customized by tapping **Clock style**. A picture from your gallery, a sticker, or even a Bitmoji can be used instead.

5. Always On Display's music info and auto-brightness can be enabled or disabled according to your desire.

Navigate to the Always On Display menu and disable the option to turn off Always On Display.

Applying Custom Themes for Always-on Display

Downloading Themes to use as your AOD is an option to consider if you are seeking a fresh AOD design. Just a heads up, you have to buy most themes.

1. Find the **Themes** tab under the **Image clock**. (To find out how to get to this stage, look at the previous ones.)

2. If you go to the **AODs** page, you can see all the available themes and buy them.

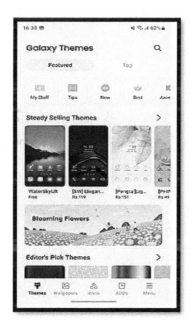

3. Press the **Menu** tab to apply a paid or downloaded theme.
4. Select **AODs** by tapping on **My Stuff**.
5. Just choose a theme for your AOD and hit the **Apply** button.

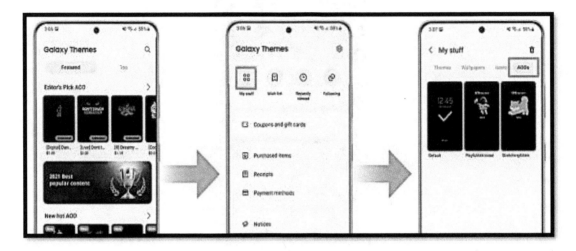

CHAPTER SIX

SECURITY

Numerous solutions exist for protecting and safeguarding your device, but preventing unauthorized individuals from accessing it is among the most effective. You can make your smartphone safer by enabling security features like face recognition, fingerprint scanners, and others. It is essential to have this in mind.

How to enable Face Recognition

When a screen on a smartphone is locked, users can unlock it using face recognition technology. At the same time, you can't use face recognition to access your device without first creating a PIN, password, or pattern. **The following are some key points to think about while dealing with facial recognition:**

- Make sure the camera lens is clean and that you are in a well-lit location before you start the facial recognition feature registration procedure.
- Using facial recognition to unlock your smartphone isn't as secure as using a PIN, password, or pattern (**note:** this implies that someone or anything that looks suspiciously like you may theoretically get access to your device).
- Under some conditions, facial recognition may not work as well as it should. Some examples of this kind of person are males with long beards, women with heavy makeup, and guys who wear hats.

The following steps are required to activate facial recognition:

- **Biometrics and Security** can be accessed via the Settings page. When you do this, the screen you see in the picture below will appear.

- Hit the link for Face Recognition. Holding the phone up to your face will be asked of you. You can see the recognition displays in the picture down below. They are efficient.

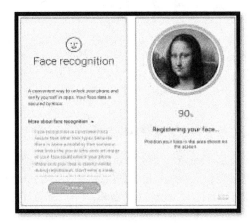

- On the final screen, you'll be asked to indicate your preference for quicker face recognition, if you want to guarantee that your eyes are open, and whether you want the screen to automatically brighten in low light. Of course. Press the **"Done"** button if you're ready. Your face is now a part of your phone.

Quick and easy, the face recognition works like a charm. It unlocks your phone so quickly and easily using facial recognition that you could think you've inadvertently disabled the lock screen, leaving your phone completely exposed. It may take you a few checks before you realize your phone is lightning-quick and very intelligent. Get rid of the selfie you have saved on your phone if it continues to annoy you.

Managing Face Recognition

Several methods are described below that can be used to adjust the accuracy of facial recognition according to your preferences:

- **Face unlock:** You can activate or deactivate the security feature that employs facial recognition using the face unlock function.
- Remove all previously saved faces and their associated data.
- **Stay on the Lock screen until you swipe:** If you're using face recognition to unlock your phone, you'll have to wait until you can swipe the screen before you can get beyond the lock screen.
- Facial recognition technology can only identify your face while your eyes are open, so remember to keep them open if you want it to work.
- Use this feature for faster facial recognition if that's what you're after. To make it far more difficult to unlock your phone using a photo or video of someone who looks like you, you can increase the security level by disabling this option.

- **Increase the screen's brightness**: To make your face visible in low-light settings, you can: Raise the screen's brightness: and temporarily raise the screen's brightness level to a higher level.

How to use the Fingerprint scanner

A secure and hassle-free way to unlock your phone is by using its fingerprint sensor. A few hurdles must be surmounted before this can transpire. For your phone to recognize your finger—which can be any finger you like—you need to show it enough views of it. In addition, it is quite particular about the fact that a fingerprint must have been saved by you. You can save many fingers on your phone. Feel free to use any finger you choose. If you'd rather not use a password to secure your device, a fingerprint recognition scanner is always an option (**note:** you can also use this function to access your Samsung account and some applications). To utilize fingerprint authentication or open certain apps, you have to go through the same process as setting up facial recognition: provide a PIN, password, or pattern.

This is the procedure:

1. Select **"Lock screen"** from the **Settings** menu.
2. Select the **Screen Lock Type link**.
- **You will need to input your security pattern.**
3. Put in your passcode.
4. Press the link for Fingerprints.
- **It brings up the screen on the left side of the picture down below.**
5. The screen will display a fingerprint symbol; press it with your finger.

Once you reach 100%, you must continue to proceed following the on-screen instructions. As you continue to cover the sensor, move your finger, and press firmly, the screen in the center of the picture below will become bored of telling you what to do. You will reach full strength in no time.

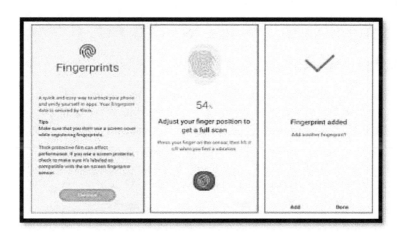

Under the Biometrics and Security link in Settings, you'll find the option to add more fingerprint sensors. Most of us can add up to nine fingerprints. You can now access your home screen with a single tap or swipe since your fingerprints are stored in memory. Have a go at it. What a smooth ride!

Fingerprint Management

In fingerprint management, new fingerprints can be added, old fingerprints can be renamed, and registered fingerprints can be removed.

1. Navigate to the **Biometrics and security** area in the **Settings menu**, then choose **Fingerprints** to access the following settings.
   - You can scan your fingerprint to see whether it has been entered in the system previously by selecting the **"Check added fingerprints"** option.
   - To add your fingerprint, go to the **"Add Fingerprint"** menu and follow the on-screen instructions.

Fingerprint verification settings

Instead of utilizing any other means of authentication, certain programs allow you to use fingerprint recognition:

- **Always-on fingerprint scanning:** This function lets you scan your fingerprint whenever you want.
- You can easily use your fingerprint to unlock your smartphone whenever you need to use it. Just use the **"Fingerprint unlock"** option.
- When the smartphone is unlocked, show an unlocking animation: It's OK to show an animation when performing fingerprint verification.
- **To show the symbol even while the screen is off:** Show the icon for the user's fingerprint whenever the screen is turned off.

How to connect your device to your PC

Connect Galaxy S24 to PC via USB

Just plugging in a USB-C connection is the simplest method to link your Galaxy S24 to a computer. To connect devices with PC cases that have a USB-C connection on the front, you will likely want a USB-A to USB-C cable. Note that you should use a cable that is rated for rapid file transmission. Although most manufacturers' offered cables are adequate, Samsung's includes a USB-C to USB-C connection, which is unusual. There are several reliable choices available for those who want to move huge files between their computer and Android phone.

Galaxy S24: Connect to PC via Bluetooth

Bluetooth is another option for connecting your phone to your computer. Even if your S24 supports Bluetooth 5.0, the PC you're using could be using an earlier version. You can forget about getting lightning-fast data transfers if that's the case. Having said that, Bluetooth is more of a luxury than a necessity.

How to pair the S24 with a personal computer over Bluetooth is as follows:

1. Launch the PC's **Settings** app.
2. To access **Bluetooth & Devices**, click on that option.
3. Select **Add device**.

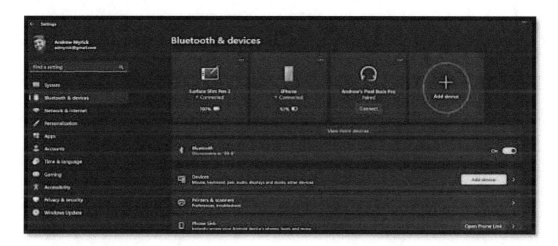

4. Choose **Bluetooth.**

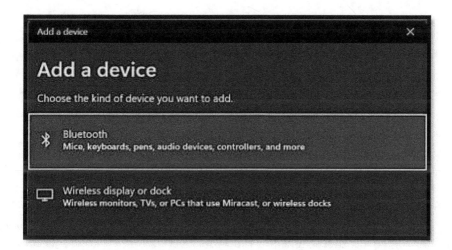

You can go on to your S24 now that you've finished with the PC part of the procedure. Please follow these steps to complete the connection.

1. Take a look at your Galaxy S24's **settings menu**.
2. Press on **Connections**.
3. At the very top, tap on **Bluetooth**.
4. Go to the **Available Devices** section and look for your computer.
5. If your computer appears in the list of devices, tap on its name.
6. Verify that the pin on your personal computer corresponds to the one on your S24.
7. Choose the **OK** button.

Connect Galaxy S24 to PC using Link to Windows (Phone Link)

Another option for connecting your Galaxy S24 to your computer is to use the built-in program. After a few years on the market, Your Phone has become compatible with both Apple's iOS and Google's Android. On the other hand, Android offers superior integration. Samsung has teamed with Microsoft to pre-install the Link to Windows / Your Phone on several of their newest handsets. Products such as the Galaxy S20, Galaxy Note 20, and, of course, the Galaxy S24 fall within this category. Follow these steps to set up your phone. Verify that your Galaxy S24 is both powered on and linked to Wi-Fi before proceeding. Installing Link to Windows is the first step.

1. Just enter **"Your Phone"** into the taskbar search box on your computer.
2. Pick **Your Phone** from the list of options.
3. Select **Android** as the smartphone model.
4. Go ahead and click **Continue**.
5. Sign in to your Microsoft Account page.
   - Verify that the Microsoft account you're using on your computer and phone is the same.
6. To finish setting it up, just follow the on-screen directions.

If you'd rather not use your computer to initiate the procedure, you can do it on your S24 instead. The necessary steps are as follows:

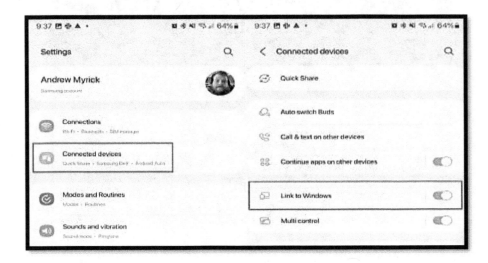

1. Open the Galaxy S24.
2. To access the **Notification Shade**, just swipe down from the top of the Home Screen.
3. You can access all the notification toggles by swiping down once more.
4. Press the **Link to Windows**.
5. Use the Microsoft account you use on your computer to log in.
6. Press **Allow Permissions.**

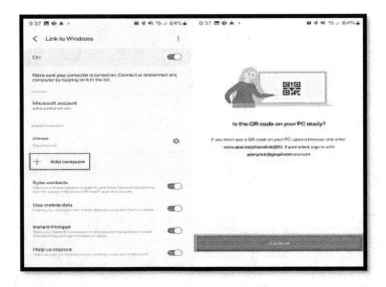

Assuming everything is OK, the Notification Shade will show your computer's name under the **Link to Windows.**

Samsung DeX and how to enable it

Every single Samsung Galaxy smartphone comes equipped with Samsung DeX. Important for enhancing multitasking capabilities, this feature lets you link your device to a TV or PC. **The available functionalities that can be used with this feature are as follows:**

- Install Samsung DeX on your computer for effortless and rapid file transfers.
- Make a WiFi connection or use an HDMI cable to connect to a display device such as a TV or monitor.
- Even after you've transferred Samsung DeX to your TV, you can keep using your phone. The device in question can also serve as a trackpad if you prefer that option.

To utilize DeX to its full capacity, you'll need a USB-C to HDMI cable and, maybe, an extra set of input devices. Sometimes, you can just wirelessly cast your screen to a TV that supports it, so an adapter isn't even necessary. Additionally, you can use a USB cord on a Windows PC to launch DeX as an app on your computer. However, this step completely removes the benefit of using your phone as a computer. You won't need any advanced IT skills to do the task.

How to use Samsung DeX with an HDMI monitor

Connecting your Galaxy device to a HDMI display with a USB-C to HDMI connection is the simplest method to transform it into a PC.

1. Connect your Galaxy device to the computer or mobile device using the USB-C end of the cord and the display using the HDMI end.
2. When asked, hit **Continue** and **Start** after unlocking your phone.

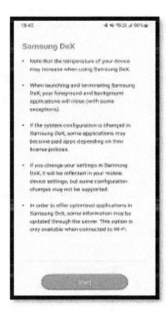

3. To access Samsung DeX, open the notification tray by scrolling down from the top of the screen. This will allow you to see your phone's screen on the external display. Press the **Start** button to confirm.
4. The DeX interface, which the phone displays, resembles a desktop OS and appears on your monitor. The app tray can be accessed by the icon in the bottom left corner of the screen, while the notification tray can be found in the lower right corner.

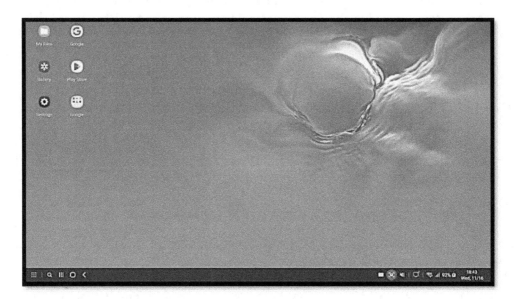

5. Launch the notification tray and press **Use your phone as a touchpad**. For input, use your phone's touchscreen.

6. After you're done using DeX mode, save your settings and then disconnect the HDMI wire. Another option is to exit DeX by clicking the Apps icon in the bottom left corner and then clicking Exit DeX.

How to use DeX wirelessly with a compatible TV

You can use DeX without an HDMI connection if your TV is compatible. Only Samsung Smart TVs and TVs manufactured in 2018 or later and equipped with Miracast functionality are compatible with Wireless DeX. **If your phone and screen are compatible, you can connect them like this:**

1. To access the **Quick Settings** panel on your mobile device, use your finger to scroll down from the top of the screen.
2. Press **DeX**.
3. Select **DeX on TV or monitor**.
4. Select **"Allow"** when asked.

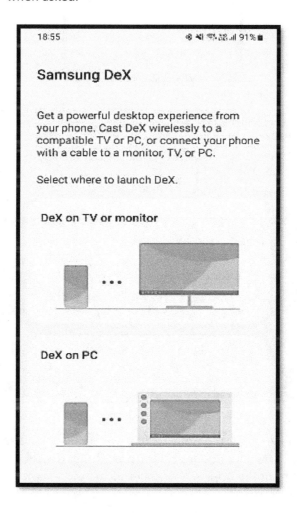

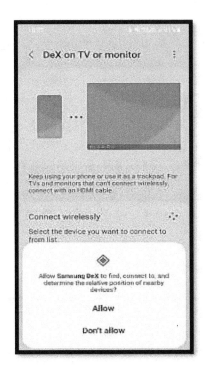

5. Pick out a TV or monitor to cast to.
6. Press the **Start** button.
7. The DeX interface, which resembles a desktop OS, is shown on your TV via your phone. The app tray can be accessed by the icon in the bottom left corner of the screen, while the notification tray can be found in the lower right corner.

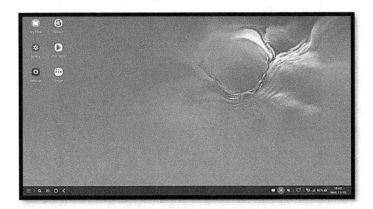

8. When you open the notification tray on your phone, you'll see an option to utilize it as a virtual touchpad (**Use your phone as a touchpad**). Tap on it.
9. Select **Exit DeX** from the **Apps** menu that appears in the bottom left corner to exit DeX mode.

CHAPTER SEVEN

MULTI-WINDOW AND S PEN

About Samsung Galaxy S24 S Pen

You can express yourself creatively with the built-in S Pen on the Galaxy S24 Ultra variant. New features, including auto-formatting and text cleanup, are compatible with the regular Air command menu and Air actions, and this upgraded S Pen is no exception. If you're feeling creative, you can use the screen of the S24 Ultra to make art while it's switched off, or you can join PENUP sketching contests. With the S Pen, you can easily take screenshots and snap fast images with the Camera app.

Pair and charge the S Pen

When you connect your S24 Ultra S Pen to your device, it will instantly link and charge. You can even link an S Pen Pro and reset the connection if necessary.

1. To access the S Pen, go to the **Settings** menu, then hit **Advanced features** and select **S Pen**. Notably, you can also detach the S Pen from your device, enter the Air command menu by tapping its symbol on the right side of the screen, and then hit the **Settings** button at the bottom.

2. The screen will prominently display the battery percentage of your S Pen.
3. After you hit the three vertical dots (More options), you'll have the option to reset your S Pen. After that, connect it by inserting your S Pen.

Use Air command and Air actions

The S-Pen on the Galaxy S24 Ultra is compatible with Air commands and actions, much like the S-Pens on earlier models.

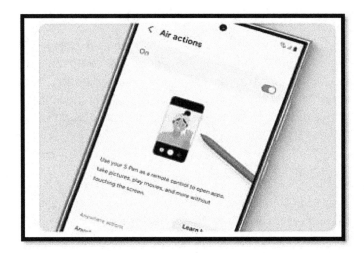

Taking the S Pen out of your device and tapping the pen icon (Air command) on the screen's right side will bring up the Air command menu. You can do a lot more with the Air command options, such as translating text, making notes in Samsung Notes, scribbling on the screen, and enlarging text. By touching the + symbol (Add) at the bottom of the screen, you can add options to the menu. Then, choose the S Pen feature and app you want. By using air actions, the S Pen can be used to do tasks just by gesturing. The S Pen can do a lot of things, including control the camera, play music, and launch applications. Press the S Pen icon after going to Settings and choosing Advanced features, to alter these options. Choose Air actions, then choose Anywhere actions, App actions, or General app actions to choose your preferred options.

Write with the S Pen

The S Pen to-text feature, which can convert your handwriting into text instantly, is probably already known to you. The S Pen and Galaxy S24 Ultra have upgraded this feature, making it even better with options for translation, auto-summarizing, spellchecking, and auto-formatting driven by artificial intelligence. Your handwriting can be neatened using the new Clean up feature as well.

- Launch Samsung Notes, go to the app's main menu, and then, to begin a new note, hit the pencil symbol.
- Start writing with the S Pen. At the bottom of the screen, you should see the Clean up or convert to text icon, which looks like a pencil with a wand. Tap on it. Press on Convert to text after that.

- A text-to-handwriting converter will appear in a pop-up window. If necessary, you can inspect and compare your original handwriting by swiping right on the pop-up.
- To save the transformed text to your note, use the "Add to note" button.

Note: You can also copy the note or utilize the three sparkles symbol (Notes assist icon) to access features like Auto format, Summarize, Correct spelling, and Translate.

- You can easily correct slightly slanted handwriting. After you've finished writing with the S Pen, you can clean up your handwriting by tapping the button that says Clean up or convert to text again.
- To automatically clean up the writing, you can press the checkbox, or you can select Settings to bring up the options to straighten, align letters, evenly spaced words, and fix the shape of letters.

Note: The **Settings icon** is located next to the current language. To change it, tap on it.

Color and create artwork

With the Galaxy S24 Ultra S Pen, you can do more than just write; you can also draw. For instance, you can discover a wide range of works and artists using PENUP, Screen off memo, or Samsung Notes to draw on your device's screen even while it's turned off. If you want to color, sketch, and share your creations with the world, PENUP is where you need to be. Press the pen icon (Air command) on the screen's right side to bring up the Air command menu; from there, choose PENUP. After you verify your age, you'll be able to proceed with the required permissions. You can access the Drawing, Photo drawing, Coloring, Live drawing, and Challenges options from the PENUP welcome screen. In addition to seeing the artwork of other users, you can also upload photographs using the Gallery app.

Capture photos and screenshots

Take pictures and Screenshots with ease with the S24 Ultra S Pen. In the Camera app, you can use the button of the S Pen as a remote control, and you can capture a screenshot of the current screen using the Smart Select option.

Control your camera remotely

1. To configure the S Pen to use as a camera remote, go to the **Settings** menu, then touch on **Advanced features**. Finally, hit on **S Pen. Press Air actions**, then if necessary, press the top switch to activate Air actions.
2. To activate the camera, go to the app's settings and swipe to the General menu. If it isn't already on, hit the button next to Camera.

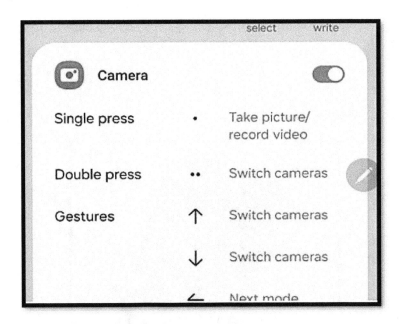

3. Choose "T**ake picture**" after tapping the option next to "Single press."

Note: Keep in mind that if you'd rather not utilize the feature, you can choose **"Do nothing"** instead.

4. Launch the **Camera** app, choose **PHOTO**, and finally, snap a photo by pressing the **Pen** button on the S Pen's side!

Capture your screen with Smart select

1. To activate Smart select, go to the **Air command** menu by tapping the pen symbol on the screen's right side. From there, press **Smart select**. To draw a rectangle or oval around the content you want to capture, choose the capture option you choose.
2. You can utilize extra options like Pin, Copy, Auto Select, Draw, Extract text, and Share once you capture the screen.

3. At the end of the process, touch the **Save** icon.

CHAPTER EIGHT
KEYBOARD

While the Galaxy S24's screen is crucial, the QWERTY keyboard will likely be where you spend the most time typing data.

Using the software keyboard

When the program senses that the user needs to type anything, the virtual keyboard appears. The picture below shows the keyboard, which is located at the bottom of the screen.

Use one-handed option

After the keyboard appears, choose the icon for the one-handed keyboard. Depending on your taste, you can shift the keyboard to the left or right by selecting the arrow icons. At any time, you can use the expand icon to make the keyboard fit the whole screen.

Use Swype

With Swype, you can choose a word and move your finger over the screen to choose it, letter by letter. The text area will be auto-populated with words.

Auto-complete suggestions

The top of the keyboard will display three options as you type a word. To input the selected proposal, just click on it.

Access emojis, audio messages, capitalize text and symbols

After finding the option you want, choose it.

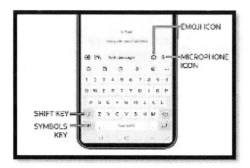

- **EMOJIS:** Find and click the emoji symbol.
- **SPEECH-TO-TEXT:** To use the speech-to-text feature, select Microphone.
- **CAPITALIZE TEXT:** Press the Shift key to capitalize the text.
- **SYMBOLS:** To access the symbols, use the Symbols key.

Note: By pressing the 1/2 key on the Symbols keyboard, you can access more symbols.

How to Configure Samsung Keyboard

Select the Settings icon to view the Keyboard settings while the keyboard is shown. Altering the keyboard's layout, height, and smart typing capabilities are all possible under the settings menu.

Note: If you want to change your keyboard settings without opening the keyboard app, you can do so by swiping down from the notification bar, and then tapping the settings button ⚙. From there, go to general management, and finally, tap on Samsung Keyboard settings. The default Samsung Keyboard's greatness lies in its adaptability. In addition to language, layout, themes, size, and feedback, you can also add your symbols. Access the Samsung Keyboard settings on your Samsung mobile device by navigating to **Settings > General Management > Samsung Keyboard settings.**

Set Samsung Keyboard as your primary input method. You cannot access it otherwise. Select **Default Keyboard** from the **Keyboard list and default** menu in **General Management** if you haven't already. **The Style and Layout** menu has submenus that you may use to personalize your keyboard.

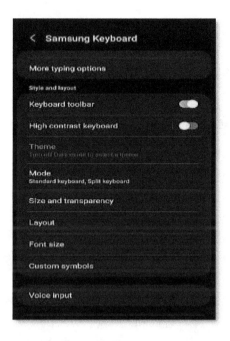

The contents of each sub-menu are as follows:

- **Keyboard themes**: Light, Solid light, Dark, Solid dark, and Color palette are available. If you have your system display set to dark mode, they won't operate. To open the notification panel in its entirety, use two fingers to swipe down the screen. Next, turn it off.
- **High-contrast keyboard**: As part of its eyesight-enhancing features, Samsung has included a high-contrast keyboard with four different levels of contrast. You can notice keyboard components better with their help.
- **Modes**: Switch between a standard, one-handed, and floating keyboard under the "Modes" menu. You can switch between portrait and landscape orientations.
- **Size and transparency**: Drag the sliders to change the keyboard's size and position, and also toggle its transparency. Only in floating keyboard mode can you adjust the transparency.
- **Keyboard font size:** You can change the size of the letters and symbols on the keyboard by dragging a slider.
- **Keyboard layout**: To change the keyboard layout, you can do things like enable alternate characters and have the number keys appear above the letters.

- **Custom symbols:** Replace the quick access symbols associated with the full stop (.) near the space bar.

Steps to change the keyboard theme on your Samsung Galaxy S24

Modifying the Samsung S24's keyboard theme is as easy as following these steps:

- Pull up the App drawer and go to **Settings**. The primary settings will be shown on your Samsung Galaxy S24.
- Find **"General management"** while scrolling and touch on it. The screen where you can alter the features and other services of the device will open.

- Choose **Samsung Keyboard settings**. On the next screen, your device will display the options to alter the theme of the keyboard.

- Locate **"Theme"** by scrolling down and tapping on it. The various keyboard themes will be shown on the screen. Light is the default theme for you.

- You can change the theme of the keyboard by simply touching on one of the available options; doing so will instantly alter the appearance of the keyboard.

To return to the original style, however, just press the high-contrast keyboard to activate the high-contrast keyboard theme. More options will be available to you if you complete this change. After you turn on the high-contrast keyboard, you can choose a theme to use. An excerpt will appear at the screen's base. That covers the basics of customizing the Keyboard Theme on the Galaxy S24.

How to use Samsung Voice Input

To save customers the trouble and energy of having to type, Samsung has included voice input as a very helpful feature for its Galaxy smartphones. Consequently, people may choose to speak aloud rather than write with their fingers daily. Choosing this option is much more convenient. You can enable the Samsung device's voice input feature using the Samsung keyboard. Once you reach your location, continue speaking the information you want captured by selecting the Voice input option from the menu. Start by opening the **"Settings"** app. Locate the **"General Management"** option by scrolling down the Settings menu. There are several device-specific options under the **General Management** menu. Navigate to **"Samsung Keyboard Settings"** and press it.

Hopefully, you've reached the Samsung Keyboard Settings page now. You can activate voice input by tapping the **"Voice Input"** option after scrolling through the options. By default, the Voice Input option is set to "**None**." The Samsung Galaxy S24 usually has two options for voice input: **"Samsung Voice Typing"** and **"Google Voice Typing."** You can choose the one you like most by pressing on it.

The Voice Input feature on your keyboard will be activated after you choose either Samsung Voice Typing or Google Voice Typing. You can use it in any program that allows you to enter text, such as chat or note-taking apps. A symbol representing a microphone should now appear on your keyboard. The Voice Typing feature can be used by tapping on the microphone icon.

To speak what you would have written, just touch this symbol. A brief moment of thought occurs on the phone's screen before it announces that it is listening. Feel free to begin speaking. You can either wait quietly or press the **Done** button when you are finished. Your recent statement will be shown to you in just a few seconds! To save time and effort while writing messages or text, you can enable voice input speech to text. It's a simple and basic method. You can make full use of this helpful feature by following the provided instructions.

How to use Emergency mode

If you own an Android smartphone, there are several options for extending the life of its battery. Switching to emergency mode is one of those things. The Samsung Galaxy S24 has an emergency mode, and this guide will show you how to activate it. Keep reading for a more in-depth description of this feature, as well as instructions on how to activate it and understand how it works on your brand-new Samsung smartphone.

What is Emergency Mode?

With Samsung Galaxy phones, emergency mode is an integrated feature. Ensuring consumers have easy access to crucial functionality during emergencies is its primary design goal. As soon as you turn it on, it will lock down your phone, removing everything except the most necessary applications and capabilities. All of your important contacts, as well as your phone and messaging apps, are part of this.

What to do before enabling Emergency Mode

Before turning on emergency mode on your Samsung Galaxy S24, there are a few things you should think about doing so that you will be completely ready for any emergency circumstance.

1. **Set up your emergency contacts:** Verify that your emergency contacts are current and that you have added them to your phone's contact list. In case of an emergency, you can readily reach them by calling or messaging them.
2. **Charge your phone:** You should still ensure that your phone is well charged before using emergency mode since it is meant to save battery life. This will make sure that in case of an emergency, you can utilize the necessary functions thanks to the ample battery life.
3. **Enable location services:** In the event of an emergency, location services can be helpful since they enable emergency responders to swiftly find you. Verify that your phone's GPS is active and that location services are enabled.
4. **Manage/adjust your emergency mode settings:** The functions accessible in emergency mode can be adjusted to meet your requirements. You can customize the message that will be delivered to your emergency contacts and choose which applications to include in emergency mode, for instance.

How to Enable Emergency Mode on Galaxy S24

It is easy to put your Samsung Galaxy phone into emergency mode. You can go on with these steps if you've fulfilled all the conditions:

- **Step 1:** The first step is to go to the power options menu by holding down the power button for a few seconds. Press and hold the button until the power menu appears.
- **Step 2:** In the power options menu, choose or touch Emergency.
- **Step 3:** When asked, read the text that follows and then press Agree to accept the terms and conditions.
- **Step 4:** Choose the people you want to add as emergency contacts. In case of an emergency, you can also provide medical records or any other pertinent material.
- **Step 5:** Personalize the emergency mode settings so that you can use the functions you desire, such as the flashlight or internet.
- **Step 6:** At last, to put your Galaxy S24 into emergency mode, touch Enable.

When you put your phone into emergency mode, it will restrict access to just the most necessary applications and capabilities.

Emergency mode features

In case of an emergency, your phone will restrict access to certain applications and services. The purpose of this is to save battery life while still providing you with the necessary functions during an emergency. Swipe down from the top of the screen and touch on the Emergency mode symbol to open the options for when you need to go to emergency mode. In case of an emergency, you can utilize the following features. While in emergency mode, just a handful of applications on a Samsung Galaxy phone can still be used. You can rely on these applications in case of an emergency.

In case of an emergency, the following Samsung applications will continue to work:

- **Phone app** – An app that lets you contact local emergency services or someone you've designated as an emergency contact in the event of a crisis.
- **Messaging app** – The messaging app lets you share your current position and a pre-written message with people you've designated as emergency contacts.
- **Camera app**–You can capture images and movies with this camera app, which might come in handy in case of an emergency.
- **Flashlight app** – To help you see in low light, there's an app that lets you utilize your phone's flashlight.
- **Internet app** – If you need to look anything up or get in touch with the authorities in an emergency, you can use this online app.
- **Settings app** – The Settings app gives you access to the device's emergency mode settings and lets you update them if necessary.
- **Compass** – Using the compass can help you get back on track if you ever get lost.

What happens when your phone is in Emergency Mode?

In case of an emergency, you can maximize the standby duration of your Galaxy S24 by switching it to emergency mode, which will enable it to preserve the battery for as long as possible. To help you get the most out of your phone's battery life, this feature when turned on, will dim the screen and disable several features. To save power use, the system interface, and the home screen, in particular, will switch to a dark theme. In this mode, you can still use the phone app and other essential features, such as making emergency calls to a designated number. You will still be able to communicate your location details via text since the messaging features remain functional. In this mode, you can also use the flash and sound alerts, among other useful features. But keep in mind that not all Samsung applications will work when in emergency mode. For instance, to save battery life and make sure that only necessary applications are accessible, they will block social networking apps, gaming, and any other non-essential programs.

When to put your phone in Emergency Mode

As a handy feature, emergency mode on Samsung Galaxy phones can be utilized in many different scenarios. **Here are a few typical situations when you may need to activate emergency mode on your phone:**

1. **Natural disasters**: Essential elements like emergency contacts, a flashlight, and internet connectivity to acquire scenario updates are crucial during natural catastrophes like earthquakes, storms, or floods.
2. **Medical emergencies:** With emergency mode, you or someone you're close to can easily access medical information and emergency contacts in the event of a medical emergency.

3. **Safety concerns:** When you're in a risky or harmful situation, you can make sure your emergency contacts know where you are and access important services like location sharing and SOS texting by enabling emergency mode.
4. **Power outages:** By switching to emergency mode, you can save power and still have access to functions like a flashlight and emergency contacts in case of a power outage.
5. **Traveling**: Having emergency mode turned on can make it easier to reach emergency services, share your position, and send an SOS message if there is an emergency when traveling to a new or unfamiliar region.

Exit Emergency Mode on Galaxy S24

If you own a Samsung Galaxy phone, turning off emergency mode is as simple as turning it on. For the Galaxy S24 follows these steps:

- **Step 1:** One must first press and hold the phone's power button until a menu of power options appears.
- **Step 2:** To disable or exit emergency mode, press the corresponding button (Disable/Exit).

Alternatively, you can disable or turn off emergency mode by touching the three dots in the top right corner of the screen. From there, you can choose those options. When the confirmation box appears, press Disable to finish. After that, your phone will return to its regular mode, leaving emergency mode behind. The Samsung Galaxy S24 Emergency Mode ends there.

CHAPTER NINE
CAMERA APP

You need to launch the Camera app before you can snap a photo. Using the Application list to open the Camera app is the standard method. To open the app, just touch the camera icon .

How to Navigate the Camera Screen

The Camera app allows you to take stunning photos and videos using your device's rear and front cameras, respectively. **For several methods to navigate the camera screen, you have the following options:**

1. Start up your device's camera app and use your finger to tap the screen to focus the camera's lens.
2. A brightness scale will show up on the screen as you finish step 1. To change the brightness, you need to drag the slider.
3. Selecting the rear or front camera is as simple as tapping the symbol to the right of the capture button.
4. Select one of the several shooting modes by swiping left or right on the screen.
5. Open the **Camera app** and choose the **Settings** option to modify the camera's default settings.
6. Hit your device's **Capture button** to take a picture.

How to Configure Shooting Mode

Make a few fundamental settings that characterize the scenario you will be shooting in by adjusting the mode setting. In Photo mode, the default is a single picture. As you can see in the picture below, the options linked to the MORE link are shown when you slide this symbol to the left. Even more shooting modes and settings are available in the Camera app on your S24 device that you can experiment with. As an example, you can use Single take to record many clips at once, and Food mode to magnify your favorite foods. You can use the on-screen tutorials or voice commands to take the photographs you want if you want some help. Just switch on Shot suggestions. You can make your beloved images and GIFs seem even better with the built-in AI Image Enhancer. Portraits will seem brighter and moving pictures will seem clearer thanks to this AI's improved resolution and sharpness, which is achieved by reducing unnecessary background noise.

The Gallery app also has a customized tales feature that you can utilize while viewing your memories. Your media files will be automatically curated and transformed into tales by an algorithm. After that, you can use carefully selected Spotify playlists to set the mood for the narrative.

Several picture and video options are brought up via the controls at the top of the viewfinder:

- **Pro:** Rather than letting the camera decide what to do, you can access all sorts of settings that a skilled operator would like to adjust in this mode. Among these settings are the exposure, shutter speed, white balance, lens length, ISO sensitivity, and color tone. This is not the mode to use if you are unfamiliar with these words.
- **Single Take:** It's almost cheating to use the Single Take feature, but it's so awesome. When you choose this option and press the shutter button once, the camera will automatically select the optimal lens and setting based on all of your preferences. What makes it so good at picking the right one? Because it is so intelligent, the S24 can figure it out.
- **Night:** When you switch to the Night mode, your camera will capture images even in the darkest conditions imaginable.
- **Food:** Capture photos of food that showcase its vibrant hues to make your pals green with envy (or hungry).
- **Panorama:** With the panorama option, you can capture a broader view than with a single shot. Press the Camera button as you spin through your selected field of view. The program then digitally combines the different photographs into a single wide-angle shot.
- **Super Slow-Mo:** To slow down very rapid photos, you can use the "Super Slow-Mo" feature, which puts you into video mode. What makes this even more remarkable is that your S24 does this in full 4K resolution, meaning you get the best of both worlds—rapid frame rate and great resolution—without sacrificing either—except maybe the space on your memory card!
- **Slow Motion:** Just plain ordinary slow motion, nothing fancy. It remains awesome.

- **Hyperlapse:** To make a time-lapse movie, just utilize this preset. As the phone moves, the video camera will change the frame rate accordingly.
- **Portrait Video:** You can approach within a few feet of an item using the Portrait Video preset. It is too much for the standard autofocus to manage.
- **Director's View:** This is a great choice: the Director's View. Choose this option if you want to make good videos. The additional lenses appear as thumbnails beside the viewfinder view of your movie. You can now creatively switch between the wide-angle and telephoto lenses while shooting.

How to use the Space Zoom feature

The Samsung Galaxy S24 Ultra has an impressive 200MP quad back camera, 100x Space Zoom, and great Nightography or low-light shooting capabilities. As its name suggests, the Samsung Galaxy S24 Ultra's Space Zoom feature allows you to capture high-resolution moonscapes without resorting to a tripod or additional magnification lens.

1. Get the Galaxy S24 Ultra's camera app open.
2. Verify that the Photo option is chosen.
3. Adjust the photo's frame to center the moon or make it look the way you want.
4. Scroll down to the viewfinder and tap the 10x button.
5. Press the 30x button in the menu that shows up above the Shutter button.
6. You can go even closer by tapping the 100x button.
7. Zooming in and out will be a little shaky, but if you can maintain eye contact with the moon for a few seconds, the Super Steady stabilization will kick in (you can use the in-picture aiming frame to help you concentrate).
8. A yellow in-picture frame will appear while stabilization is active, indicating that the aim is steady and easy to manage.
9. Press the shutter button after allowing the AI-assisted camera to focus on the moon.

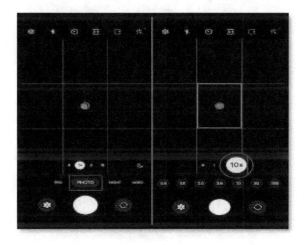

Upon activating the 30x digital zoom, a preview window will be shown in the upper right corner. The purpose of this is to illustrate the relative positions of the moon and the lens. Furthermore, even when you zoom in 100x, it will still be in the upper right corner.

How to take pictures

It will just take a second or two for you to snap a photo after you launch the Camera app. Take the screen as your very own viewfinder. A picture similar to the one below shows what you see on your screen.

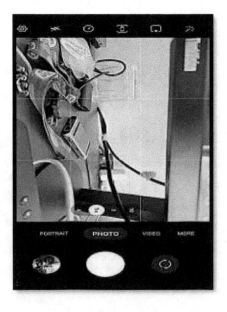

Also, what's the best way to take a picture? To activate the digital shutter, just press the large white button⬜ located on the device's right side. What you see via the viewfinder becomes a digital copy of it. A smaller percentage of the battery is used by this screen compared to previous technologies, but it is still substantial. Even higher power savings with Super AMOLED are available with darker backgrounds.

How to record videos

All you have to do to snap a photo is launch the Camera app. But you're keen on filming it. Swiping the Photo link to the left (in landscape mode, that is, down in the image below) will launch the video.

On the viewfinder, you'll see four distinct icons:

- **Record Button:** The Record button can be found in place of the shutter button.
- **Video Stabilizer:** With the help of some digital wizardry, the Video Stabilizer makes it seem as if you're effortlessly gliding the phone from one spot to another. Turning off this feature will make the video choppy and unwatchable. Keep the Video Stabilizer turned on for most situations. People who see it will love it.
- **Auto Framing:** This feature will automatically adjust the camera's focus to capture all of the subjects. You won't have to worry about the social consequences of severing a friend's arm. If you want to be able to manage what's on the screen, it might potentially be somewhat frustrating.
- **Video Format:** Access a plethora of choices for picture resolution and frames per second with the help of the "Video Format" menu item.

Pressing the Record button🔴 is all that's required to begin. The still picture in your viewfinder transforms into a moving picture, and the button that used to be the record button now appears as the pause or stop indicator⏸️⏹️. You can pause the recording and resume it at a later time.

By pausing, the video remains unchanged. After saving, it returns to the Record button. The creation of a new file with each subsequent recording is usually not a problem.

How to use Director's View

You can use both the back and front-facing cameras to capture footage simultaneously with the director's view! At the same time as you respond to things around you, you can record them.

Dual recording with the front and back cameras gives extra alternatives, particularly for vloggers, as Director's View lets you record from several cameras simultaneously. Those looking for entertaining, educational, or conversational material can find more to their liking in dual-recorded vlogs.

How to shoot Director's View

- **Step 1:** Head over to the **camera**.
- **Step 2:** Go to the list of shooting modes and choose **MORE > DIRECTOR'S VIEW**.

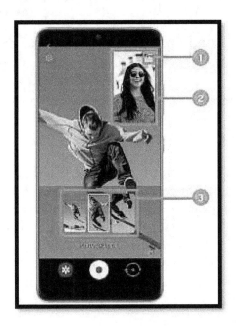

① Change the screen mode   ② Front camera view   ③ Camera thumbnail

- **Step 3:** Choose the desired camera thumbnail.
- **Step 4:** Choose a screen mode from the three options (Split view, Single view, and Picture-in-picture) by tapping the symbol for **"Change the screen mode"** in the top right corner.

① PIP View
② Split View
③ Single View

- **Step 5:** To start recording a video, press the **Record** button. By touching the thumbnail, you have the option to switch the camera while recording. To reveal the thumbnail, use the Display button if it is hidden.
- **Step 6:** When you're done recording, hit the **Stop** button●.

How to use Zoom-in mic

While recording audio in Video mode, you can boost the volume and reduce ambient noise by **focusing closer to the source. You can't utilize this function with the front camera or any other video mode.**

1. Press Settings from the **Camera** menu.
2. Then, activate the **zoom-in mic** by tapping on the **Advanced recording options**.

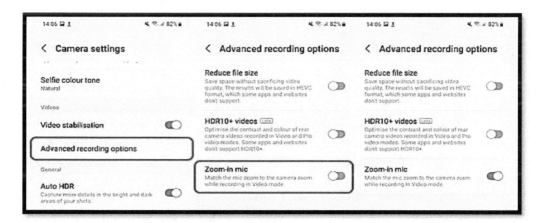

3. Go back to the main screen of the Camera.
4. Go to **Video** Shooting Mode by swiping left.
5. To start recording, tap the **Record button**.
6. You can zoom in or out on the audio source by bringing your fingertips together or apart on the screen. If an amplification is turned on, the microphone symbol will show you the level applied.

List of Camera settings and their functions

You can access a few shooting modes directly from the viewfinder. Starting from the viewfinder and working our way clockwise around the screen, we have

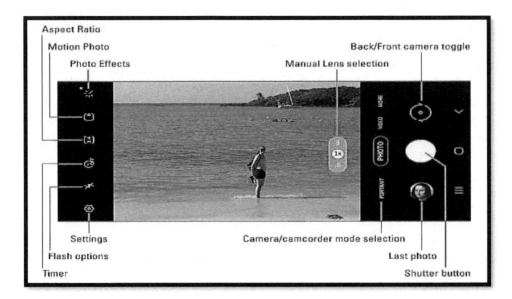

- **The viewfinder:** This is where you can preview the final image. This may seem like stating the obvious, but it's one method to adjust the magnification. Within the viewfinder, you can pinch or extend the screen to zoom in or out.
- To zoom in, stretch the screen.
- Zoom the view out by pinching the screen.
- **Lens Selection:** Pinch to zoom out, or extend to zoom in. Another alternative is to use one of the available lenses. The 3 in the image above represents a telephoto lens with a magnification of 3x, the 1x in the circle represents a normal lens with a magnification of 1x, and the .6 represents a macro lens. The many Galaxy S24 models vary in this respect. How many lenses are on the front and rear of your device depends on its model and whether you're taking pictures using the rear or front-facing camera. Depending on the lenses you're using, the amount of choices shown will vary. If you own an S24 Ultra, here is where the additional expense is worthwhile.
- **Rear-facing camera to front-facing camera toggle:** Pressing this symbol will switch between the two cameras, one of which is a respectable 10-megapixel shooter. Seeing the final product before you take the photo makes this a great choice for selfies, as previously said. The front-facing camera on the S24 Ultra is a behemoth with an incredible 40 megapixels.
- **Shutter button:** The symbol that snaps the image is the shutter button.
- **Gallery:** To see the photos you have recently taken, tap this button.

- **Camera/Camcorder mode:** This is crucial. The ideal starting point is likely to be in Photo mode as seen in the image above. You have a really intelligent camera, and the photo mode is very effective at figuring out how to enhance your shot. On the other hand, you can tweak the parameters to make it seem more sophisticated. Switching to video recording is likewise done in this way.
- **Settings:** The next section goes over the fancier settings that are available in the Preferences menu.
- **Flash options:** You should still learn how to handle your flash, even if you're going for a minimalist approach. A flash is an essential photography accessory. Taking pictures of some animals, babies, or fish in an aquarium are examples of situation when a flash might be helpful, but is forbidden. (Do you recall the fate of King Kong?) No matter what, you can always control the flash with your phone. Above the viewfinder, you should see the Settings symbol; tap on it. You can choose between turning the flash off, turning it on, or using the built-in light meter to determine whether the flash is needed using the Auto Flash option. In the image below, you can see all of the examples.

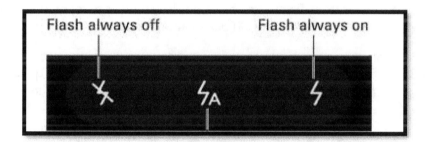

- **Timer:** This feature allows you to get a group shot by delaying the shutter button's action by a few seconds.
- **Aspect Ratio:** The conventional picture size is 4 by 3 units in height, which is known as the aspect ratio. A 4:3 aspect ratio is what this indicates. This is the usual, but why stick to the same old thing all the time? You have a variety of choices to experiment with.

CHAPTER TEN
GALLERY

Using the Gallery app  on your Galaxy S24, you can view media files. You can also make tales or organize your media by album. Enjoy more than just picture viewing with the Galaxy S24 Gallery app. You can also use it to create albums and narratives out of your images. Additionally, the Gallery app has a built-in picture editor that you can use to edit your photographs. After shooting a large number of images with their Galaxy S24, most users seldom find the opportunity to manually edit and organize them. Insightful and automated picture management is possible inside the Gallery app, thanks to its recognition of location, time, scene, and people.

How to view images in Gallery

You can admire your flawless selfie or film, the result of an hour of practice, on the Gallery app. A variety of filters, effects, and styles are at your disposal for use in picture and video editing.

1. Press the **Pictures** tab after opening the **Gallery** app. Press the **Search** button in the top right to look for a certain image or video. Look it up using the album name, a tag, or anything else you can think of.

2. Press an image to see it in. Just drag the screen to the left or right to see different files.
3. Utilize the choices located at the base of the screen to designate an item as a favorite, make edits, read details, share, or remove it when you've discovered the perfect picture or video.

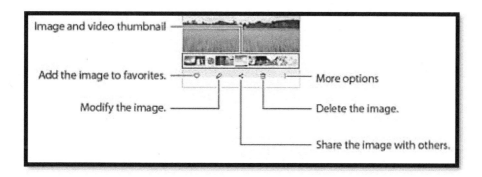

Image and video thumbnail

Add the image to favorites. ————○ ⭘ < 🗑 ⋮———— More options

Modify the image. ————————————————— Delete the image.

————— Share the image with others.

4. If you want to print or set the image as a wallpaper, you can do so by tapping **More Options** (the three vertical dots).

How to Edit Pictures

The S24 series of cameras are top-notch, offering a wide variety of shooting modes that can capture breathtaking images. And if that weren't enough, there are a plethora of editing tools at your disposal to ensure that your final products are flawless. Locating the desired picture in the Gallery is the first step. To access further editing options for this picture, you can find them at the bottom of the screen. It looks like a pencil silhouette; to see it, hit the Edit button ✎ (see image below).

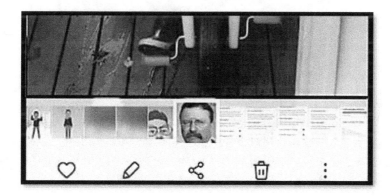

Here are a few choices:

- **Slideshow:** Each picture is shown for a brief moment in this mode. Not only can you choose the transition speed, but you can also add music and choose from many picture transitions.
- **Crop:** To crop a picture, select it and then remove any unwanted or distracting elements. When the software detects an item, it will enclose it in a virtual box. The box can be repositioned inside the picture, but its size cannot be changed. The next step is to decide whether to keep the cropped picture or delete it.

- **Set As:** Choose this picture to use as your background or to add as a contact's image.
- **Print:** If you've connected a local printer to your phone via Wi-Fi or Bluetooth, you can print using this option.
- **Rename:** You can flip the picture horizontally or vertically using these choices. If you swivel the camera to capture a higher angle and then decide you prefer a landscape orientation, this feature will come in handy (or vice versa).
- **Details:** Check out the image's fixed and immutable metadata for all the information you need.

How to play a video

From the viewfinder screen, you can access the video you just created or recorded by tapping the Gallery icon. Next to the Record button in the viewfinder, you can see the Gallery symbol. As shown in the picture below, tapping it opens the Gallery app.

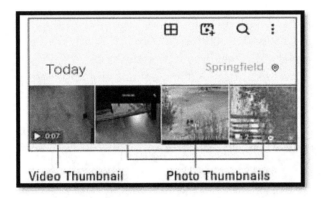

In addition to the other current photographs, this also pulls up the video. The videos can be distinguished from the images by their play icon■, an arrowhead pointing to the right, and the information about the video's runtime. The video in question here lasts for seven seconds. Currently, you are presented with many options. Pressing the thumbnail will open the video player. The thumbnail will be magnified to fill the whole screen. Simply tap the "Play Video" link, and the video will begin playing. Video viewing on a mobile device is just as enjoyable as looking at still images.

How to use video enhancer

It is well-known that Samsung's proprietary skin atop Android has a plethora of functions. The Video Enhancer is a neat function that you should try out. This function might improve your Samsung phone's experience if you watch a lot of movies or TV episodes. You can manually toggle the functionality on or off. So, it's easy to disable if you're not a fan of its features. In addition, the function is compatible with a wide range of apps, so you can enjoy entertainment on the go. The default video player, YouTube, Prime Video, Netflix, and Hotstar are all compatible.

The functionality can be enabled on the Samsung S24 smartphone by following these steps:

1. Open your phone's **Settings** menu.
2. Find the **Advance features** option halfway down the page and touch on it.

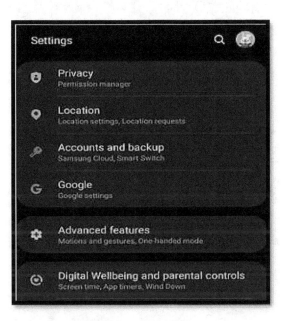

3. Toggle the **Video Enhancer** option on when you scroll down. Toggle it on and off with a simple touch.

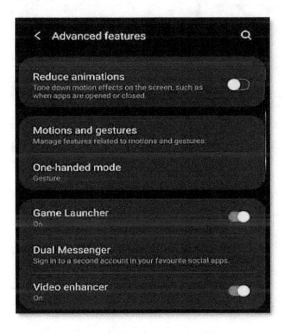

Furthermore, you can see the compatible applications by tapping on Video Enhancer. Your phone's installed applications are the ones that appear on the list.

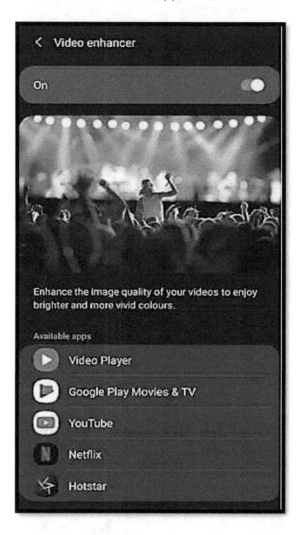

It follows that you should see an improvement the next time you use any of the applications on the list. The screen's brightness will automatically rise, and the colors will be somewhat more vibrant.

How to share videos and pictures

Simultaneously, it is worthwhile to share an excellent video. Holding down on the thumbnail will allow you to share your video. The top left corner of every thumbnail is suddenly adorned with a white circle. After you tap the circle containing the desired file, a checkmark will show (see the figure below for reference).

At this point, you can either delete it or share it. You use the share option because this is so worth sharing. As seen in the figure below, this activates the sharing screen.

This is the same screen that is used for sharing images. Posting high-quality films to social media platforms shouldn't be delayed. Among the many things it will check when you hit the Share button is your preferred degree of privacy. If you agree to everything, your video will be made public.

How to delete videos and pictures

Your phone's photo library isn't perfect. You could find that you delete more photos than you end up keeping. For those of us used to high-priced cinema, this is a challenge. But soon enough, you'll have much too many pictures—and that will be the point. Select the picture you want to remove by pressing and holding it. The image-selected checkbox will pop up in a second. On top of it, you can see the Share and Delete buttons. Choose Delete if you want to remove this picture. This is your intention, as the camera can see. The picture disappears after you confirm.

Just touch on each picture you want to remove to make them disappear if you'd like to remove more. If the picture has a green checkmark, it is chosen. Before hitting Delete, tap away. A confirmation will be sent to you once. These photographs will be permanently deleted if you tap again.

How to group similar pictures

There are many different types of photos and movies stored on our smartphones. The Gallery automatically generates albums for many media formats, including Camera, Screenshots, WhatsApp Images, Downloads, and more. On the other hand, there are instances when we don't want to erase images from an album because there are too many that appear identical, and it becomes difficult to discover other photos. "Samsung Gallery create group feature" works well under these circumstances. You can arrange your phone's Gallery by grouping similar photographs. **This will make them simpler to discover later or just make them appear better overall. Follow these steps to create photo sets:**

- Launch the **Gallery** app on your mobile.
- Go to the Albums menu by tapping on **Albums** and then tap **More** options (the three vertical dots).
- Finally, choose **Create Group**.

- Submit the name you'd want your group to be known by.
- Press the **"Create"** button.

- After creating a new group, you can add albums to it by opening it and tapping the **Add Albums** button.
- Choose the album that you want.
- Hit the **Add** button once you're done.

Taking a screenshot

To take an image of what's now visible on your screen, you can use the screenshot feature. (Note: Most devices have a specific folder where screenshots are stored). One step in capturing a screenshot is navigating to the area of the screen you want to capture. The next step is to depress the side button and the volume down button with your fingers before releasing them. A palm swipe motion is one of the alternative approaches that can be used with the Galaxy S24. While this is a sophisticated setting, it needs to be enabled by default. The Settings app also gives you the option to manually toggle it on and off. To activate this, just run your finger down the screen to capture a screenshot.

1. You can capture palm swipes by opening the Settings app and then navigating to **Advanced Features**> **Motion & Gestures** > **Palm swipe to capture**.
2. The next step is to activate the function.
3. Once you've enabled the feature, taking a screenshot of the current screen is as easy as dragging the edge of your hand diagonally across the screen, going from side to side. Just make sure you stay in touch with the screen at all times.

Galaxy S24 screenshot: scrolling screenshot

If you want to capture an image that won't fit entirely on your screen, such as a lengthy Facebook post, you can use this screenshot feature. If you want to save a lot of time, there's an alternative to taking several screenshots and sending them all at once or piecing them together manually. A scrolling snapshot, which records the whole screen as you scroll down, is an option on the Galaxy S24. It's essentially a lengthier screenshot. You can only get the option to take a **scrolling screenshot by using one of the two techniques mentioned earlier; otherwise, it will be hidden under a toolbar button that appears when you create a conventional screenshot.**

- **Step 1:** Use one of the aforementioned ways to capture a screenshot.
- **Step 2:** The second step is to get the screenshot toolbar, which appears next to the thumbnail, and then click the Scrolling screenshot button. It is within the confines of a square, two arrows point downward.
- **Step 3:** Once you've gathered all the necessary information, keep clicking the scrolling screenshot button.

How to screen record

- Get the Quick Settings panel up and running. Just use your two fingers to swipe down from the top of the screen to do it. Then, choose the screen recorder by tapping on it. Go to the Quick Settings panel and add your screen recorder icon if it isn't already there.
- Pick an option—Media sounds, No sound, or Media sounds and mic are some examples. Select "Start recording" once you're ready.
- Your smartphone will begin recording the current screen content as soon as the countdown finishes.

- It is possible to include oneself in the recorded video. The front-facing camera is available here. It all starts with tapping the front camera icon, which looks like a human. Then, a little window will pop up, and you can begin recording your screen.
- If you want to spice things up, try writing on the screen while you record. Select the color you want to use with your finger, then tap the Pencil symbol. S-Pen is another option for writing on the screen of the smartphone. You are unable to use this screen to engage with media, games, or menu items simultaneously with your writing.
- To end your drawing, just touch the pencil symbol. The screen will return to its original state after you disable the Pencil function. Right here, you can keep recording.
- Just hit the Stop symbol when you're done recording. You can find the video in the Gallery. To retrieve some screen recordings, open the My Files app, then go to Internal storage, and finally, touch on the DCIM folder.

How to adjust the Screen Recorder

Sound, Video Quality, and the Selfie Video Size are all customizable. To adjust the screen recorder's parameters, follow these instructions.

- Click on the **Settings** icon.
- Choose **Advanced features**.

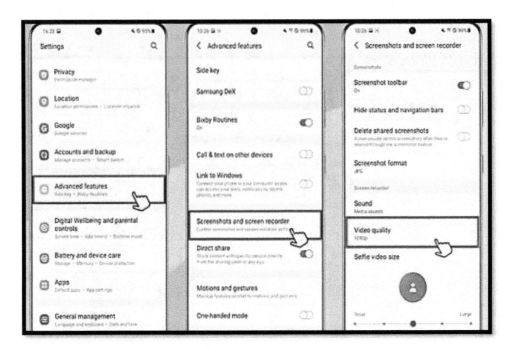

- Choose **Screenshots and Screen recorder**.
- Adjust each setting as required.

CHAPTER ELEVEN

PLAYSTORE

Google primarily caters to Android phone users via the Play Store that it sets up and runs. Installing an app on your phone is like installing software on your computer. In each scenario, a brand-new piece of software (app) improves your efficiency, makes your life easier, and/or provides endless (and often free) entertainment. A fair bargain.

Getting to the Store

The Play Store is accessible via the web via the dedicated app on your Galaxy S24 phone. If you're using a Galaxy S24, the Play Store app is your best bet for accessing the Play Store. Below, you can see the icon.

In the Apps list, you should be able to locate the Play Store app if it isn't already on your Home screen. Just press the symbol to open it. A screen similar to the one below will appear when you touch the Play Store icon;

The featured applications and the Home page will update daily to reflect the availability of new apps. Google also invests significant resources into figuring out how to make it easy for the 3.1 million applications available for Android to be discovered by the hundreds of millions of users. It is not an easy process. A few of those people have a ton of experience and are quite clear about their needs. Some are here for the first time, while others are just looking around to see if anything catches their eye.

Installing and Managing an Android App

Using the Facebook app for Android as an example, let's walk through the steps of locating and installing an app to make it more concrete.

Add this app by following these steps:

1. Press the Play Store icon and make sure the Offering category is for Apps.
2. Type in Facebook into the Query box.

A menu similar to the one below will appear when you do this. Several results include the term "Facebook," as is seen from the search results. Apps containing the term "Facebook" occupy the remaining lines in the Apps section. The majority of them, 112,160 to be exact, are for applications that improve Facebook in some manner. Choose the one that has the Facebook emblem instead of going through each one individually.

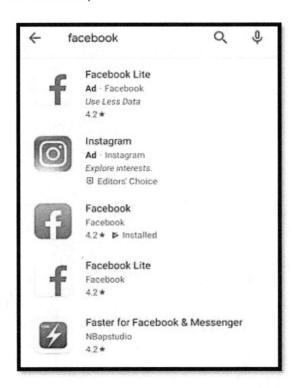

3. Press the Facebook icon.
4. Press the Install button, which is dark green.

The app's download progress is visible to you. Once the program is fully downloaded, the installation procedure will start. Most applications will display a pop-up window at some time to alert you of the data that they will be using from your phone. The purpose of this is to provide you with a general notion of the potential privacy impact of this software.

5. Choose the dark green Open button and press it.

Rating or Uninstalling Your Apps

One way to keep the Android community strong is to provide feedback on apps. You should be truthful while rating applications. On the other hand, you might ignore it and make use of the ranking system that other people have set up. You get to decide.

Following these steps will ensure that your app-related voice is heard:

1. Launch the Play Store.
2. Press the icon (the circle with your initial) that represents the Google Play Menu.

A drop-down menu appears when you do this.

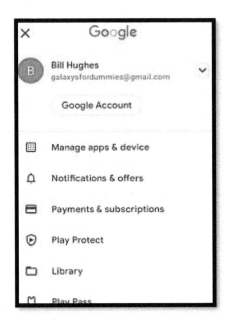

3. Press the link for Manage Apps & Device.

The screen seen in the picture below will pop up. You would want to manage, even if the Overview information is good.

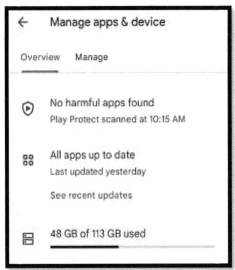

4. **Tap the Manage link.**

On occasion, a screen displaying a complete catalog of your phone's installed applications may emerge, and the Manage screen will open to see it. Look around a little more. Eventually, you will see each one. If you have a large number of applications that need updates, the Manage page may instead open to the Updates Available screen. (Sometimes, it may lead to games.)

5. **Press the Installed link.**

You can rate or delete these programs by tapping on one of them. Please give the app five stars if you find it to be excellent. Let me clarify: if you want to give it one star, touch the star on the left. Press the star on the far right to give it a perfect score of five stars.

How to Create and Use Folders

You can create folders for your app shortcuts in your Apps list to help you manage your apps. This is a detailed tutorial:

1. **Selecting and Highlighting Apps:** To begin, go to the Apps list and choose an app shortcut. After selecting one, you can add it to another app's shortcut by dragging and dropping it. During this process, you will see that the app you have selected gets highlighted, indicating that you are going to create a folder.
2. **Creating the Folder:** Let go of the app after it is highlighted. A folder will be created when you do this, and you'll have the opportunity to personalize it with these options:
   - **Folder Name:** Be sure to give your folder a unique name. You can quickly recognize what's inside thanks to this.
   - **Palette:** The folder's color can be changed to suit your tastes or make it stand out if you so choose.
   - **Adding More Apps:** You can expand the number of applications in the folder by adding new apps. Select the applications you want to add, and then click the **"Done"** button.

3. **Dismissing the Folder:** To return to the previous screen or close the folder, just press the **"Back"** button.

Your applications will be much easier to discover and use if you divide them into folders. It's an easy approach to personalizing your Apps list according to your tastes.

How to Add a Folder to a Home Screen

The Home screen can have a folder copied to it.

- Press and hold an Apps folder then press **Add to Home**.

How to Remove a Folder

Removing a folder from your Apps list is an easy way to make room for new ones. Just do as instructed:

1. **Locating and Holding the Folder:** To start, go to your Apps list and locate the folder you want to delete. Press and hold the folder once you've found it. Doing so enters a selection mode, which signifies that you are going to make edits.

2. **Deleting the Folder:** When you right-click on the folder, a menu with several choices will pop up. Find the setting that reads "Delete Folder." Press on it when you've located it. Once you click "Confirm," the system will ask you to confirm the deletion.
3. **Confirming Deletion:** Please acknowledge the deletion request to confirm your choice. By taking this precaution, you are assuring yourself that you want to delete the folder and everything in it. To avoid unintentional deletions, it's a precautionary step.

The folder and any shortcuts to its programs will disappear from your Apps list after you approve the deletion. Once again, you'll have easy access to each program's shortcut since they'll be back where they were in the Apps list.

App Settings

The Apps area of the Settings menu is where you can find all of your device's customization options. Here's a rundown of the steps and possibilities:

1. **Accessing the Apps Section:** Locate the "Apps" option in your device's Settings menu. To access the Apps area and manage your app options, tap on it.
2. **Personalization Options:** There are several ways to tailor your experience once you reach the Apps area. Some options that you might consider are:
   - **Select Default Applications:** To set an app as the default for common tasks like making calls, sending messages, and browsing the web, utilize this option. In this method, you can assign certain applications to specific actions.
   - **Samsung App Settings:** Find out how to change the settings for Samsung apps. To get the most out of Samsung-exclusive applications, adjust these settings to suit your tastes.
   - **The Apps You Use:** Select the app you're using to see and change its privacy and use settings. Remember that there are a lot of personalization choices available across applications. You can go back to the previous app settings by going to **"More options"** and then choosing **"Reset app preferences."**

Take note that you can adjust your device's behavior and application interactions to some extent with any of these settings.

CHAPTER TWELVE
CALENDAR AND CLOCK APP

Samsung has announced that their regular Calendar app is receiving an update. Improved sketching capabilities, better-shared calendar management, and better settings for dark and light modes for Samsung's smartphones and tablets are just a few of the new features featured. The most recent update to the Samsung Calendar app was unveiled at the South Korean Samsung Community Forum. The drawing in the app has been improved with the latest release. When you long-press the S Pen on the calendar, whatever form you make will be transformed into the right shape.

This is similar to what is currently available in the Samsung Notes app. Samsung has announced that, in addition to the phone's UI options, the Calendar app now offers a dark/light option. Another option is to let the app switch between light and dark modes depending on the phone's theme. You can also see entries from your work profile calendar using a Galaxy Watch that is linked to the app. No word yet from the company on whether it's limited to Wear OS wearables or whether Tizen devices are also compatible. In addition, it facilitates calendar sharing, so users can decide who can and cannot make changes to calendar entries.

The Samsung Calendar software allows you to create shared calendars using the following menu: **Calendar Settings** » **Calendar Management** » "+ **Create Shared Calendar**." Simple links allow users to send calendar invites. Permissions can be adjusted for shared calendars that are already in existence. Shortly, the updated version will start making its way throughout South Korea before eventually making its way to other markets all over the world. Hence, be sure to check the app store for updates.

Start with your calendar settings

At startup, you can choose to link your calendar with your Samsung account, Exchange (Outlook), Google, or Microsoft. After you input your email and password, your current schedules will be synchronized.

How to change your settings for the calendar

- Step 1: Press the Menu button (three horizontal lines) once the Calendar app is open.
- Step 2: Press the Settings icon.

- **First day of the week**: Any day of the week can be designated as the first day of the week.
- **Alternate calendar**: Samsung Calendar offers five other calendars to choose from. The lunar months of Hijri, Shamsi, Vietnam, China, and Korea are these.
- **Show week numbers**: You can add a number to your calendar to show the number of weeks using this option
- **Hide declined event**: You have the option to conceal the schedules that you have rejected.
- **Highlight short events**: You can quickly highlight occurrences by using this feature.

How to create events

From the Calendar app, choose the Add icon. After providing the necessary information, click on Save.

How to delete or edit an event

- **Step 1:** The first step in editing or removing an event is to access it by tapping on its date. After that, press and hold the event.
- **Step 2:** If you want to make a lot of changes to the event, choose Edit or Delete.

Edit

- **Step 1:** Open the Calendar app and choose the day you want to add the schedule.

- **Step 2:** Change the name of the event by touching the plus sign.

How to link external accounts added to synced calendars

- Go to the Calendar app's main menu (three horizontal lines) when you launch it.
- After selecting an email, tap on accounts.
- At the bottom of the page, click "Sync now."

Clock app

You can set alarms and keep track of time using the Clock app.

Alarm

Using the Alarm tab, you can set up one-time or recurring alerts and choose how you want to be notified.

1. From the Clock menu, choose Add alarm.
2. Press on these items to set an alarm:
   - Establish a timer for the alarm.
   - **Day:** The alarm days are chosen
   - **Alarm name:** Designate a name for the alert.
   - **Alarm sound:** Use the slider to choose an alarm sound and adjust the volume.
     - Vibration: You can choose to have the alarm vibrate or not.
   - **Snooze:** Get some shut-eye. You can configure the alarm's interval and repeat settings while you're sleeping.
3. Press the **Save** button to keep the alarm.

Delete an alarm

It is possible to disable an alarm that you have already set.

1. Press and hold an alarm on the Clock.
2. Hit the **Delete** button.

Alarm Settings

You have the option to set the device to vibrate in response to timers and alarms, regardless of whether the Sound mode is Mute or Vibrate.

1. From the Clock menu, choose **More Options> Settings**.
2. Press the **Vibrate** button for the alarms and timers to activate the feature.

World Clock

Find out what time it is in a lot of different cities all across the globe with the help of the World Clock.

1. Go to the Clock menu and choose **World Clock**.
2. Choose **Add City**.
3. To add a city, touch and hold the globe to spin it, and then tap on it.
   - Hold down a city and press **Delete** to remove it from the world clock.

Time zone converter

Find out what time it is in different cities across the world by setting the time in one of the cities on your World clock list.

1. Go to the Clock menu and choose **World Clock**.
2. From the drop-down menu, choose **More options** > **Time zone converter**.
3. Pick a new city from the drop-down list.
   - To add a city to the list, tap **Add City**.
4. Swipe the clock's upper-right corner to access the hour, minute, and period (AM/PM) settings. All of the other cities' local times are immediately updated as well.
   - You can bring the clock up to date by using the Reset button.

Weather Settings

On your world clock, you can see current weather conditions. Give it a try:

1. Go to the Clock menu and choose **World Clock**.
2. Go to **More Options> Settings > Show weather information** to enable or deactivate weather information.

3. Tap **Unit** to convert Fahrenheit to Celsius.

Stopwatch

To the nearest tenth of a second, you can time events with the stopwatch.

1. Launch the **Stopwatch** app by going to the Clock menu.
2. To begin the timer, tap the **Start** button.
   - To maintain tabs on lap times, tap **Lap**.
3. Press the **Stop** button to end the timer.
   - You can resume timing by hitting **Resume** after stopping the clock.
   - Click the **Reset** button to bring the stopwatch back to zero.

Timer

A countdown clock allows you to set a timer for a duration of up to 99 hours, 59 minutes, and 59 seconds.

1. From the Clock menu, choose **Timer**.
2. Press the Hours, Minutes, and Seconds keys on the keypad to set the timer.
3. After that, touch **Start** to begin the timer.
   - To temporarily stop the timer, tap **Pause**. To proceed, press the **Resume** button.
   - You can stop and restart the Timer by tapping **Cancel**.

Set a timer

A name can be assigned to a preset time, and it can be preserved. Follow these steps to complete this task:

1. From the Clock menu, choose **Timer > Add preset timer**.
2. Determine the name of the timer and the name of the countdown timer.
3. Select the **Add** button to save the timer.
   - To make changes to a preset timer that has been saved, choose **More options > Modify preset timers**.

Timer Settings

The parameters of the Timer can be altered to suit your preferences. Steps to take:

1. From the Clock menu, choose the **Timer** option.
2. The second step is to choose **More Options> Settings** from the menu that drops down.
   - **Sound:** The sound feature allows you to choose from several different pre-programmed timer sounds or to make your own.

- **Vibration:** By activating this option, you will be able to disable the vibration that the timer produces. You can see and adjust the settings for all of the Clock tools.
- The Clock menu should be accessed by selecting **More Options> Settings.**
- **Customizing service:** The customization feature allows you to modify material inside apps that have been authorized by signing in to your Samsung account.
- **About Clock:** Review the most recent software version and check for any available updates.

CHAPTER THIRTEEN
CONTACTS APP

If you want to be able to interact with anybody and everyone you could ever want to, your phone wants you to be able to do so in whatever method that you can communicate with them. Even though this is a challenging task, your Galaxy S24 makes it as simple as it can be. It would not come as a surprise to us if the technology that is included in the Contacts app ends up being one of your preferred characteristics of the gadget. In the end, the purpose of your phone is to make it easier to communicate with people you know, such as friends, family, and colleagues, and the Contacts app on your phone makes this process as simple as technology can make it.

How to create, edit, and share a contact

- When you swipe up from the main page, you will see more choices and functions that are available.
- The "Contacts" symbol, which is often shown as an address book or a person-shaped icon, should be located and selected. You will be sent to the Contacts application when you take this step.
- To begin the process of adding a new contact to your list, choose the "+" symbol that is located inside the Contacts app. It is important to keep in mind that contacts can be saved in a variety of places, such as a Google account, a Samsung account, a SIM card, or even directly on your phone.
- The field labeled "Name" will be chosen on its own automatically. To guarantee precise identification, you should type the contact's name into the keypad system.
- Please ensure that the appropriate contact information is entered into the appropriate areas. To access other fields and enter further information, scroll the screen up and click the option that says "View more."
- After you have completed the required information, you will need to click the "Save" button to complete and save the contact entry process. This guarantees that the information is kept safely and can be accessed without difficulty whenever it is required.
- If you want to return to the main screen of your smartphone without any interruptions, press the HOME key. Following the completion of this step, the process of creating contacts is complete, and you will be able to easily return to your home screen.

Importing Contact

- If you want to see all of your apps, you should start by swiping up from the Home screen. This action will bring up a menu of the applications that are currently installed on your smartphone.

- From the list of available apps, choose the "Contacts" app. Locate the Hamburger Menu, which is often represented by three lines, while you are in the Contacts app. This will allow you to access other choices.
- Select "Manage contacts" from the Hamburger Menu to begin doing actions that are associated with contacts.
- Select "Import" from the Contacts menu to import contacts into your account. To specify the source, pick "SIM." Select the contacts that you want to import, then hit the "Done" button. After that, select the destination (for example, Phone), and then click the "Import" button, followed by the "OK" button.
- To export contacts, choose "Export" from the Contacts menu. This will allow you to export contacts. As the destination, choose "SIM 1" as the option. After selecting the contacts you want to export, hit the "Done" button, then pick "Export" and then press the "OK" button.

Deciding where to store your contacts

Before going any further, you need to decide on the location in which you will save your contacts. You will find that making this decision now, using the knowledge that is provided to you in this part, will make your life much simpler in the future. Although it is feasible to merge contact databases, even the most advanced systems have their flaws. When you attempt to save a new contact for the first time, the Contacts app will immediately provide you with a pop-up screen. This will accept your first input as the choice you choose as the default once it has shown all of the alternatives that are available to you. If you want to manually switch to another of these databases whenever you save a new entry, you can do so. Be sure to decide on what you want to accomplish right now to save yourself some time and stress.

You have the following choices when it comes to where to store new contacts:

- Within your Samsung account
- Within the memory of your phone
- On the SIM card inserted into your phone
- Within your Gmail account
- As a contact in one of your other accounts

Every one of these choices comes with its own set of benefits and drawbacks. If you are merely looking for my recommendation, I would recommend that you use your Gmail account to store new contacts. If you are OK with this, go to the next part, which will discuss connecting contacts from other sources. Here is the deal: All of the available choices are equally effective if everything is functioning as it should. On the other hand, you should think about the possibilities if you constantly transfer phones, if you ever lose your phone, if you need to make substantial modifications to your contacts, or if you are frequently out of wireless service, such as when you are on an airline. Your contacts can be stored on your phone, which is the first option that was suggested. As long as you have your phone, this is an excellent choice. On the other hand, there will come a time when Samsung (or HTC, or LG, and so on) will have something that is both quicker and better, and you will get interested in upgrading. There will come a time, possibly the next year or ten years from now, when you will be required to relocate your connections to a different area if you want to maintain them. Additionally, you have the option to save your newly acquired contacts on your SIM card. You can remove your SIM card from your current phone and insert it into another phone, and all of your contacts will be transferred over to the new phone. This is one of the appealing features of utilizing your SIM card. You can easily do this if you continue to use an Android smartphone that is of a more current vintage. If you, for example, convert back to a feature phone (that is, a phone that just makes calls and texts and costs one dollar), it is nearly as simple as that. In addition, the fact that your SIM card does not need a wireless connection to update modifications is another potential benefit.

Keeping new contacts in your Gmail account is the next option available after that. In other words, your new contacts will be instantly transferred from your phone to your Gmail account on Google servers. This is what this entails. Although this retains the information on your phone, Google also keeps a duplicate of this record in your Gmail account. Changes to a contact can be made on either your mobile device or your personal computer.

The two reasons why I advocate utilizing your Gmail account are as follows:

- You can easily keep these records using your full-sized keyboard rather than the tiny keyboard on your phone.
- It is simple to retrieve all of these contacts on a new Android phone simply by informing the new phone that you have a Gmail account. As a result of the fact that you will most likely immediately log into your Gmail account after purchasing a new phone, your contacts will resurface more quickly than they would if you choose the fourth option.

Your fourth choice is to save the contacts in one of the email accounts that you already have at your disposal. If you already consider your email account, be it your personal or business account, to be the main area where you save contacts, then this could be the ideal choice for you. It is highly recommended that you make use of one of your email accounts as the default location for storing new contacts if you already have a successful database discipline with one of your email accounts.

Editing Contact

1. To begin, open the Contacts app on your device, and then tap the name of the individual whose preferences you want to modify. Tap the Edit button. To make changes to the information that is connected with your contact, you need to tap the area when you wish to make such changes.
2. After tapping the area in which you wish to enter more phone numbers or email addresses, touch the **"+ Add"** button to add the additional information.

3. To delete something from your device, you must do so by pressing the Remove button, which is represented by the minus symbol and is situated next to it.
4. Select the option **See more** to make modifications to additional parameters, such as the address, notes, and relationships, amongst other things.
5. Hit the **Save** button after you have finished making all of the necessary adjustments.

Sharing Contacts

The Contacts app gives you the ability to import and export your contacts without leaving the **app itself. If both of your devices are connected to the same Samsung Account, then your contacts will be synchronized across both of those corresponding devices.**

1. Open the **Contacts** app on your device, and then tap the name of the individual whose information you want to share with others. To share this, just click the **Share** button at the bottom.
2. Select the mode of communication that you want to use to disseminate the contact information. Either the material can be shared in the form of text or a file, depending on your preference.

It is important to keep in mind that the presentation of these options can change based on the device that you are using.

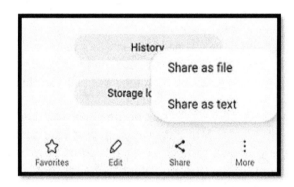

3. Once you have done so, choose the form of sharing that you like, such as Quick Share or email, and then proceed to follow the instructions that appear on the screen as necessary. Additionally, it is conceivable that to do what you want to do on the other device, you will need to choose the Import option.
4. The fourth step is to go to the screen that displays contacts, then touch and hold the contact that you want to share, and finally let go of your finger. Through this, you will be able to share a large number of contacts all at once. Following that, choose any other contacts that you would want to share with others. Alternatively, you can choose **All** by selecting the menu button located in the top left corner of the screen. Press the Share button after you have finished making your selections.

5. Proceed with the instructions that appear on the screen to import the contacts from the other smartphone.
6. You can be able to share a contact with another device if you use a QR code on one electronic device. When you want to produce a QR code for a contact, you must first touch the contact, then press More (the three dots that are vertically arranged at the bottom of the screen), and last, you must hit the QR code.
7. After that, start the Contacts app on the apparatus which is the second piece of hardware. Following the selection of "More options" (the three dots in a vertical position), pick "Scan QR code" from the submenu that immediately displays. You will need to adjust the device so that it can read the code.

Take note that you can also use an application that is capable of reading QR codes to scan the code.

Managing Duplicate Contacts

If your friend continues to get a new number, things have the potential to become complicated. **The simple act of merging their contact information will prevent their name from displaying in your Contacts list more than once due to duplicate entries.**

1. The first step is to launch the Contacts app and then tap the Menu button, which is represented by three horizontal lines.
2. Select the contacts that you wish to manage, and then go to the Merge contacts menu option.
3. If you have multiple phone numbers, email addresses, or names, you have the option of combining them. After you have chosen the repetitions, you should thereafter tap the Merge button.

Favorites

1. To add your favorite contacts, first go to the Contacts menu and then hit the option that says **"Add your favorite contacts"** at the very top of the screen.

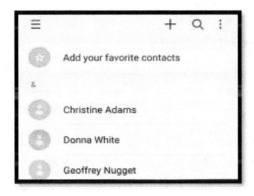

2. You can either search for the name of a certain contact or swipe through the list to find that contact. Once you have completed selecting your selection(s), you should end the process by touching the **Done** button.
3. The contact(s) that you have selected will ultimately be shown at the very top of the page, in the section labeled Favorites. Despite this, you will still be able to see their information in the general contacts list that is located below.

It is important to note that to add more contacts to your list of favorites, you must first choose a contact and then hit the Favorites symbol, which is a star-shaped icon located at the bottom of the screen. A yellow hue will be applied to the symbol to represent it.

4. In addition, you can reorganize the contacts that are most significant to you. Changing the order of your favorites can be accomplished by navigating to the Contacts page, hitting the More options button (which appears to be three vertical dots), tapping the Reorder Favorites button, and then dragging and dropping your contacts into the order that you like. Before you can begin to arrange your preferred contacts, you need to have at least two of them.
5. If you want to remove a contact from your list of favorites, all you have to do is choose the contact you want to remove and then click the Favorites button. The symbol will transform into a white version of itself.

Groups

1. Pick Contacts from the drop-down menu, then pick Menu (the three horizontal lines), and lastly select Groups from the list of available options available.
2. Select the **"Create group"** option, and then give the group a name once you have clicked on it. You can also customize the ringtone for groups, which is another choice available to you.
3. Select the individuals you want to include in the group by pressing the Add member button, and after you have completed your selections, choose the **Done** option to complete the process. Press the **Save** button.
4. You can decide to allocate freshly formed contacts or contacts that are already in existence to the newly established group at any time.

Managing Contact Storage

If you discover that you need to save the information from your phonebook in a different location, you can move it from your phonebook to a SIM card. Ensure that your smartphone is equipped with a SIM card before you begin. This is the first thing you should do before anything else.

1. Step one is to locate the **Contacts** app on your smartphone and then start it.
2. From the submenu that displays, choose **"Menu"** (the three horizontal lines), "Manage contacts," and "Move contacts" to move contacts.

3. Select the option that is most suitable for your requirements, then select the contact or contacts that you desire, and finally, submit your request by clicking the **Done** button.
4. Click the Move button after selecting the new location to which you want to send the contact(s), and then go to the next step.

How to delete contacts

- To remove a contact, you must first press and hold the button on that contact. This action will bring up a menu that has a variety of choices that are attached to the contact that has been chosen.
- From the option that displays, click either "Delete" to delete the chosen contact individually or "Delete All" to erase many contacts simultaneously.
- Once you have selected the deletion option, you will need to confirm your selection by clicking "Move to Trash" or another confirmation prompt of a similar kind. After completing this step, the chosen contact will be transferred to a folder that is either marked as trash or destroyed.
- Finally, to return to the main screen of your smartphone seamlessly, hit the HOME key from the keyboard. Taking this step brings the process of deleting contacts to a close, giving a more simplified approach to managing your contacts.

CHAPTER 13

SOUND, VIBRATION, AND NOTIFICATION SETTINGS

How to Access Sounds and Vibrations Settings

There are several different settings available to you on your Galaxy phone that will keep you informed if you get system alerts, text messages, emails, or phone calls. These notification settings can be customized according to your preferences, whether you would rather get a notice by a vibration, a sound, or through a Bluetooth audio device than any other method. Additionally, technologies such as Dolby Atmos are included among the sophisticated sound options that are available on your phone.

These parameters can be adjusted in the following manner:

Accessing Notification Settings: When you want to adjust your notification choices, you should go to the settings on your phone. Discover the section labeled "Sounds and Vibration" or "Notifications" on your device. You can then explore a variety of choices to customize your notifications from that point on.

How to Set Sound Mode

A more convenient solution is available to you if you want to adjust the sound mode of your smartphone without having to depend on the Volume controls. **To investigate this functionality, proceed in the following manner:**

1. **Accessing the Quick Settings Panel:** To access the Quick Settings Panel, swipe downwards from the top of the screen on your smartphone. This will allow you to reach the settings panel for the Quick Settings. While you are there, search for the Settings button and then press on it.
2. **Selecting Sound Mode:** The second step is to choose the sound mode by going to the Settings menu and selecting "Sounds and Vibration." Through the use of this option, you will be able to modify a variety of features of the audio settings on your device. Within this section, you will discover the "Sound Mode" category.
3. **Choosing a Sound Mode:** You can choose from the following three choices under the Sound Mode category:
   - **Sound:** This option makes all sound alerts available to the user.
   - **Vibrate:** When your smartphone is set to this mode, it will vibrate to alert you to receive alerts without making any audible noises.
   - **Mute:** In the "Mute" option, both the sound and vibration alerts will be silenced when you choose this mode.

You can quickly alter the sound settings on your smartphone without having to use the Volume keys by tapping on the option that you choose to be most suitable.

Note: If you wish to change the sound mode without impacting the customized sound levels you have set, it is necessary to utilize the sound mode choice rather than the Volume keys. By doing so, you will be able to move between different sound modes without any interruptions while still retaining the volume levels that you choose for each mode. It is possible to control the sound preferences of your device rapidly and efficiently by using this approach, which eliminates the need to go through the Volume buttons. This method guarantees a hassle-free experience that is personalized to your specific requirements.

How to Adjust Vibration Settings

1. **Navigating to Vibration Settings:** Search for "Sounds and Vibration" under the Settings menu, and then select it with your finger. From that point on, choose "Vibrate."
2. **Adjusting Vibration Patterns:** In the Vibrate menu, you have the opportunity to personalize several characteristics of the vibrations that your smartphone produces, including the following:
    - **Call Vibration Pattern:** This feature allows you to customize how your phone vibrates when incoming calls are received. By selecting a pattern that is tailored to your tastes, you can ensure that you can identify between the various call notifications.
    - **Notification Vibration Pattern:** You can personalize the vibrating pattern that is used for alerts by using the notification vibration pattern. You can then determine the sort of notification depending on the vibration in this manner.
    - **Vibration Intensity:** Control the intensity of the vibrations by modifying the intensity. This allows you to control the strength of the vibrations. The vibration can be adjusted to suit your preferences, whether you want it to be soft or severe.

As a result of making these modifications, you will have the ability to customize the vibrations that your smartphone produces, which will improve your entire experience working with it.

Note: Please take note that these options provide you the ability to fine-tune the vibrations of your device following your preferences. This will ensure that you get notifications in a manner that is most suitable for your requirements. Because of these customization possibilities, you will have a smooth and user-friendly experience, regardless of whether you want to modify the intensity of the vibrations or want to have separate patterns for calls and alerts.

How to Control Volume Levels

The level of ringtones for phone calls, notifications, media, and system sounds can be adjusted according to your preferences. To find it, swipe down from the top of the screen to reveal the Quick settings panel, and then hit the Settings button. This will allow you to access the Quick Settings panel. Subsequently, choose Sounds & Vibrations, and then proceed to select Volume.

Next, adjust the sliders appropriately for each kind of sound. The volume can also be controlled by using the Volume keys on your keyboard. When the button is pressed, a pop-up menu opens, which displays the current music genre as well as the volume level. You can expand the menu by pressing it, and then you can alter the volume of the different types of sounds by dragging the sliders accordingly.

How to Change Ringtone

You have the option of designing your call ringtone or choosing from a library of pre-programmed sounds to personalize your phone rings. To find it, swipe down from the top of the screen to choose the Quick settings panel, and then hit the Settings button. This will bring up the Quick Settings panel. Following that, choose Ringtone, followed by Sounds and Vibration. To use an audio file as a ringtone, you can either hit the plus symbol (+) or touch a ringtone to listen to a preview of it and then choose it.

How to Configure Sound for Notification Alerts

Choose an audio file for every notification update. To find it, swipe down from the top of the screen to reveal the Quick settings panel, and then hit the Settings button. This will allow you to access the Quick Settings panel. Tap the Notification sound option, followed by the Sounds and Vibration option. Tap a sound and then choose it to hear a trial version of the sound. It is important to take note that the App settings area gives you the ability to create unique notification sounds for each app.

How to Manage System Sound

You can choose a sound theme for a variety of functions, including touch interactions, charging, modifying the sound mode, and functioning with the Samsung Keyboard. To find it, swipe down from the top of the screen to choose the Quick settings panel, and then hit the Settings button. This will bring up the Quick Settings panel. This is followed by clicking on Sounds and Vibration, followed by System Sound. Take a sound from the list and choose it.

How to Set Notification Pop-up Style

Alter the apps that send you notifications and how notifications alert you to prioritize and maximize the effectiveness of app alerts. To find it, swipe down from the top of the screen to choose the Quick settings panel, and then hit the Settings button. This will bring up the Quick Settings panel. Make your selection from the Notifications menu for the pop-up style. You have the option of selecting between Brief or Detailed alerts, and then you can tailor the notifications according to your preferences.

How to View Recently Sent Notifications

Examine a list of programs that have sent notifications in the recent past. To find it, swipe down from the top of the screen to choose the Quick settings panel, and then hit the Settings button. This will bring up the Quick Settings panel. You can choose the option you wish to use under Recently sent by pressing the Notifications button. In addition, you can expand the list by pressing the More button. Any necessary adjustments to the notification settings can be made from this location.

How to Enable Alert When Phone Picked Up

Make sure that the gadget is set up to vibrate whenever you pick it up so that you are reminded of any missed calls or messages. To find it, swipe down from the top of the screen to choose the Quick settings panel, and then hit the Settings button. This will bring up the Quick Settings panel. Next, choose Advanced Features, and then select Motions and Gestures from the menu. When the phone is picked up, turn on the switch that is located next to the word "Alert."

How to Enhance Audio with UHQ More Upscale

Enhances the sound quality of movies and music, resulting in a more immersive listening experience on both platforms. Tap the Settings button after entering the Quick settings panel by sliding downwards on the screen. This will allow you to find it. Next, choose Sounds and Vibration, and then select Sound Quality and Effects from the menu. The Upscaling option can be selected by selecting the UHQ Upscaler button. It is important to note that the Galaxy Buds variants do not include this enabling feature. Corded headsets and Bluetooth-enabled devices are the only ones that are compatible with this product.

How to Personalize Sound with Adapt Sound

Enhance the quality of your listening experience by adjusting the sound specifically for each ear. To find it, swipe down from the top of the screen to choose the Quick settings panel, and then hit the Settings button. This will bring up the Quick Settings panel. Next, choose Sounds and Vibration, and then select Sound Quality and Effects from the menu. Tap Adapt sound to determine when you want to make adjustments to the sound settings, and then hit the sound profile that satisfies your preferences the most. Then, to make changes to it, hit the button marked Settings.

Note: Make sure to click the **Test My Hearing** button so that your device can determine the sound that is most suitable for you.

How to Configure Separate App Sound

An application can be programmed to play media sounds on a Bluetooth speaker or headset in a manner that is distinct from the other noises (such as alerts). Tap the Settings button after entering the Quick settings panel by sliding downwards on the screen. This will allow you to find it. Finally, choose Sounds and Vibration, and then select Separate App Sound from the menu. Tap the Turn on Now button, and then choose the appropriate settings for the App and Audio device. This will enable the Separate app sound. Having a Bluetooth device connected is required to make use of the available audio choices.

How to Activate Do Not Disturb

You can silence notifications and sounds when this mode is activated on your device. You can also arrange routine activities like sleeping or attending meetings, as well as make exceptions for certain people, apps, and alerts. Tap the Settings button after entering the Quick settings panel by sliding downwards on the screen. This will allow you to find it. The Notifications and Do Not Disturb settings can be toggled between. You can configure several different settings, including Do Not Disturb, for how long, Sleeping, Add Schedule, Calls, messages, chats, Alarms and sounds, Apps, and Hide notifications.

How to Explore Advanced Settings

Alerts for apps and services can be customized. Tap the Settings button after entering the Quick settings box by sliding downwards on the screen. This will allow you to find it. Next, choose Notifications, and then select Advanced Settings from the menu. Show notification icons, Show battery %, Notification history, Conversations, Floating notifications, Suggest actions and answers for notifications, Notification reminders, Application icon badges, and Wireless Emergency Alerts are just a few of the options available.

How to Utilize Dolby Atmos

Your Galaxy S24 provides a better audio experience using Dolby Atmos, which provides high-quality surround sound. This is true regardless of whether you are absorbed in a movie or listening to your favorite songs on Spotify. **This feature, however, is not active by default; thus, the following is a straightforward method that will show you how to manually enable it:**

1. **Accessing Dolby Atmos Settings:** To activate Dolby Atmos, you will need to go to the settings menu on your phone. You can do this by selecting the Settings app from the menu.
2. **Navigating to Sound Quality and Effects:** Once you are in the Settings menu, locate and choose "Sounds and Vibration." This will allow you to go to the Sound Quality and Effects section. In this section, you should seek the heading "Sound quality and effects."
3. **Activating Dolby Atmos:** Under the Sound Quality and Effects menu, look for the option labeled "Dolby Atmos." Select it with your finger, and you will see a toggle switch. The Dolby Atmos mode can be activated by simply toggling the switch to the "On" position.
4. **Customizing Dolby Atmos Settings:** According to the default settings, Dolby Atmos will improve the sound quality of any material that you are now listening to. When Dolby

Atmos is engaged, you can, however, further adjust. You can configure it to turn on automatically by tapping on the "Auto" option when you are doing the following:

- Watching a movie
- Listening to music
- Engaged in a phone conversation

5. **Enhancing Gaming Experience:** If you like playing games on your Galaxy S24, you should make sure that Dolby Atmos is turned on for gaming. When you play games on your smartphone, you will be able to enjoy immersive surround sound thanks to its implementation.

When you follow these instructions, you will not only be able to activate Dolby Atmos, which will result in a more immersive audio experience, but you will also have the ability to customize its activation depending on the activities that you do. Dolby Atmos improves the audio quality of your Galaxy S24, making it more enjoyable to watch movies, listen to music, have phone conversations, or play games. This feature elevates your whole entertainment experience.

How to Adjust Equalizer

You have the option of selecting from different audio presets that are suited to a range of musical genres, or you can change your audio settings on your own. Tap the Settings button after entering the Quick settings panel by sliding downwards on the screen. This will allow you to find it. Next, choose Sounds and Vibration, and then select Sound Quality and Effects from the menu. Tap Equalizer to choose a musical genre to listen to.

CHAPTER FOURTEEN
INTERNET APP

Starting the Browser

When it comes to gaining access to information from the Internet via your Galaxy S24 phone, you provide yourself with three different possibilities. Your option of which one to employ is entirely up to you. Among the options are:

- **Use the regular web page:** To use this option, you will need to visit a website by using its standard address, also known as its URL, and then the website will appear on your screen. There is a possibility that the text that is produced will be brief.
- **Use the mobile web page:** Today, almost every website provides a mobile version of their standard website page for users to access. The complete website has been condensed and shortened so that it can be read more easily on a mobile device.
- **Find out whether a mobile app is associated with the web page:** A great number of websites have discovered that the most efficient way to get the information that is available on their website is to develop a mobile application. If you intend to visit this website frequently, the software modifies the web page so that it seems more aesthetically pleasing on a mobile device's display. With this information in mind, you should go to the Internet. Your Galaxy S24 phone can provide you with a few different options on how to get there. You can go there by clicking on any one of the three icons that are in the picture below. You can begin your surfing experience by tapping any of them.

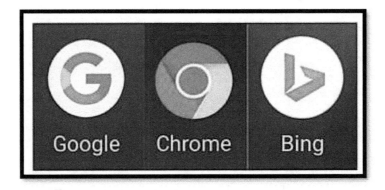

Read the sidebar that is located nearby and is dedicated to Internet terms if you would want to have a better grasp of the reasons why there are various possibilities. Depending on what you want to do, you can begin by tapping either the Chrome symbol or the Google icon. Generally speaking, these icons will be located on the Home screen. Alternatively, you can locate the Chrome or Google symbol by tapping the Application icon.

Accessing Mobile (or Not) Websites

Your phone's web browser is intended to function in the same way as the browser on your personal computer. You can input a web address (URL) at any moment by touching the text box that is located at the very top of the screen to do so. This is something that you can experiment with by entering the address of your preferred website and seeing what occurs.

To provide an example, the desktop version of the website Refdesk.com is shown on the page that is shown in the image below.

As can be seen, the whole of the website is present. It is also clear that the writing is rather tiny, as you can see. This specific website is an extreme example of a typical website since it is meant to direct you to a large number of helpful links that are located all over the Internet. However, although this writing seems clear and brilliant on your lovely screen, it is still rather little. When you are looking for the information you need, you can extend and squeeze. You can easily browse websites that you are acquainted with if you put in a small amount of effort doing so. Discovering a website's mobile version is the alternative choice that can be made. As an example, the mobile version of Refdesk.com is shown in the picture that can be seen below. Although the mobile version loads more quickly, it has fewer photos, the writing is bigger, and it is less dazzling than the desktop version.

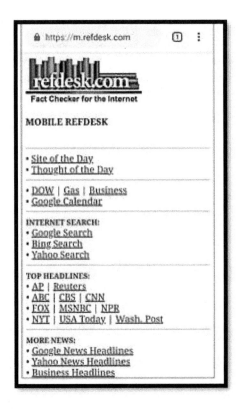

How to browse the internet

Step 1: Launch a Web Browser

- Installing a web browser application on your Samsung Galaxy S24 mobile, such as Google Chrome or Mozilla Firefox, is the first step in using the device to access the internet.
- To open the browser application, tap on the icon that appears on your home screen or in the app drawer.

Step 2: Enter a Website Address

- To enter the address of a website, you must first open the browser and then touch on the address bar that is located at the very top of the screen.
- Make use of the on-screen keyboard to type in the URL or web address of the website that you want to visit.

Example: "www.example.com" or "**https://www.example.com**"

Step 3: Navigate and Interact with Web Pages

- At this point, the browser will load the web page once you have entered the URL of the website.
- To see the content of the website, you can use your finger to scroll up and down on the page.
- When you want to interact with other items on the website, you can do so by tapping on links or buttons.

- Zooming in or out on the page can be accomplished by pinching in or out on the screen.

Step 4: Use Browser Tools and Features

Investigate the many tools and functions that are made available by the browser to improve your surfing experience:

- **Bookmarks:** Bookmarks allow you to save webpages for easy access at a later time.
- **Tabs:** To make it simpler to switch between several tasks, open numerous web sites in separate tabs.
- **History:** View a list of websites that you have visited in the past by clicking on the History tab.
- **Settings:** You can customize the settings of your browser, including the homepage, privacy preferences, and other settings.

Step 5: Perform Searches

- The majority of web browsers are equipped with a search bar or an integrated search engine that allows users to do searches.
- To search, you must first touch on the search bar, then enter your search query, and then either press the search button or click the enter key.

Step 6: Manage Cookies and Privacy Settings

A more tailored surfing experience can be achieved via the use of browsers that have options to control cookies and privacy settings:

- **Clear cookies**: You can clear cookies by removing cookies that have been saved for websites that you have visited.
- **Manage site permissions**: For websites, control access to the location, camera, microphone, and other aspects of the device.
- **Incognito mode**: The anonymous browsing mode allows you to browse the web without preserving your browser history or cookies.

How to check and change between tabs

- On your device, launch the Internet browser or the Samsung Internet browser program.
- Look for an icon that looks like two squares or a tab icon, which is often found toward the top of the screen that you are using.
- To see all of the tabs that are currently open, tap on the icon.

CHAPTER FIFTEEN

MESSAGES APP

Sending the first message

Two outcomes can occur while texting. The first instance is when you send a text message to someone for the very first time. The second instance is when you engage in a discussion with a person in a text message. It is quite simple to send a text message to your closest buddy when you first obtain your phone when you are ready to boast about your new Galaxy S24, and when you want to send a text message to your best friend.

1. **Select the Messages icon**  **from the Home screen**

The emblem for Messages seems to be a speech bubble from a comic strip that has been squared up and placed inside a blue circle. When you touch it, you will be presented with a Home screen that is mostly empty for messaging. The space starts to get more crowded if you have a few talks going on.

2. **Select the icon for "New Message."**

When you tap the symbol  **that looks like a new message, the screen that is seen below appears;**

3. **Tap to enter the recipient's ten-digit mobile telephone number.**

There is a text box that appears at the top of the screen, and the To field is located at the very top of the box. At the very bottom of the screen is where you will find the keyboard. The field at the top of the page is where you should input the telephone number, as seen in the figure below. The position of the numbers on the keyboard is along the top.

Even if the person you are messaging is someone who lives in your immediate vicinity, you should still mention the area code. The addition of a 1 before the number is not required in any way. If this is your very first text, you have not yet had the opportunity to accumulate a collection of texts. After you have been using your messaging app for some time, you will have input your contact information, and your phone will begin to attempt to predict who you wish to send the message to. You have the option of following one of its recommendations, or you can just continue typing.

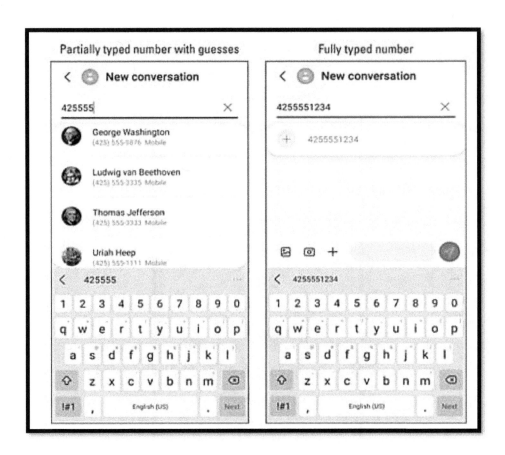

Partially typed number with guesses — Fully typed number

4. **To type your text message, tap the text box that says Enter Message.**

The text box that is located to the right of the paper clip symbol will be where your message will be displayed. Including punctuation and spaces, the maximum number of characters that can be included in a text message sent using the Android Messaging app is 160. The program keeps track of the quantity of characters that are still available to a user.

5. **Send the text by tapping the Send button** 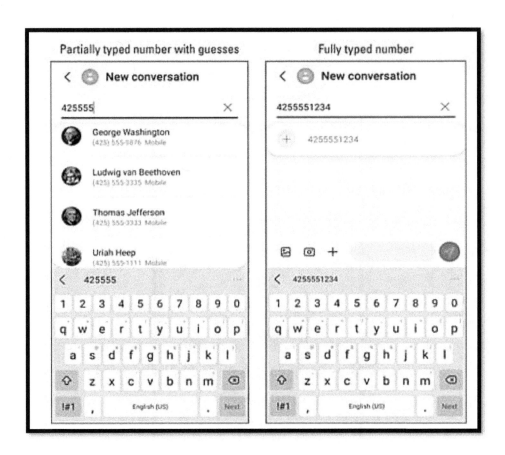 **to the right of your message.**

Before you begin typing, the Send button is not visible on the screen. Following the completion of a text entry, a blue-green circle with the outline of a paper aircraft will transform into a blue-green circle. If you touch the blue-green button, the phone will handle everything else from this point on. It just takes a few seconds for the message to be sent to the mobile device of your buddy. You can begin entering a name in the recipient text field or touch a name from the contact list after you have completed the process of building your contact list. When there is just one number associated with a contact, your phone will presume that the phone you wish to send a text message to is the one that is receiving the message. Whenever that contact has more than one phone number, it will inquire as to which of those numbers you would want to send your text message to.

Carrying on a Conversation via Texting

In the days before the Galaxy S, the majority of mobile phones would maintain a record of the messages that you sent and received. Regardless of who sent or got the messages, the phone maintained the sequence in which they were sent or received, regardless of who sent or received them. Texts that are kept sequentially are ancient. Your Samsung Galaxy S24 can preserve a record of the contact with whom you have been exchanging text messages and keeps a conversation record of each set of texts that you exchange with them. You can see that the initial page for messaging keeps track of talks by looking at the picture that is provided below. If you begin messaging someone, all of those messages will be compiled into a single conversation. Each text message is shown in the order that it was delivered, with the orientation of the text bubble indicating who the author of the message is.

There is a text box labeled "Enter Message" located at the bottom of the screen. Any text that you enter can be sent to the person with whom you are now having a chat thanks to this useful function. When things were more difficult, it was often difficult to keep track of the several texting discussions that you were having at the same time. There is a second communication that takes place whenever you start a texting chat along with another individual. Very quickly, you will find yourself engaged in several different discussions. Be not concerned. These are not the kinds of talks that you need to keep going on and on forever. If you don't text for a time, no one will give you a second thought.

How to Forward Messages

1. **Launch the Messages App:** Start the Messages app by clicking on it. You can do this by choosing the Messages app from the Home Screen or by browsing the applications screen and taking the appropriate action.
2. **Navigate to the Desired Message:** Using the Forwarding option, locate the message that you want to send to another individual and then click on it.
3. **Long Press on the Message:** First, you will need to press down on the message for a considerable amount of time until a menu appears on the screen.
4. **Select Forward:** From the menu that opens, choose the "Forward" option.
5. **Select Recipients:** Please select the contact or contacts to whom you would want to share the message.
6. **Click Send:** Pick the recipients, and then click the "Send" button to send the message to them. To send the message, you must first pick the recipients.

Receiving Text Messages

Texting someone is a simple process, but receiving one is even simpler. If you are having a text discussion with someone and they send you a new text message, your phone will vibrate and/or beep to let you know that they have sent you a new message. A very small version of the Messages symbol is shown in the notification section of the screen, which is located at the very top of the screen. Two options are available to you: either you can launch the messaging program or you can drag down the notification area from the very top of the screen. It is up to you. Any attachments that are received are shown on the discussion screen if they are received.

Managing Your Text History

You can keep track of all your messages on the Messaging Conversations page until you decide to remove them. From time to time, you should clear this screen. Pressing the Menu icon, followed by Delete, is the quickest way to manage your messages. The talks you want to remove can be selected and deselected in this way. By tapping the trash can symbol located at the screen's base, you can make them vanish. To start a new discussion is another way to delete. The text can be deleted by pushing and holding the balloon. In a few while, a menu will show up where you can remove the message. Having a large number of texts makes this process much slower. I suggest you go brutal with erasing the previous discussions and messages. Deleting all of your old messages can be a relief.

How to Send SOS Messages

Having a safety net in place is vital in case you face difficulties or meet potentially harmful conditions. Setting up your device's SOS message function is one efficient method for doing this.

To enable this vital feature, follow these steps:

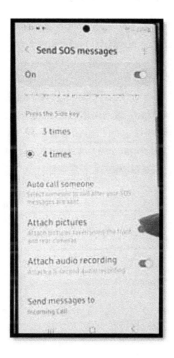

1. Launch the Settings app from your device's home screen or the quick panel to begin the procedure.
2. Go to "Safety and emergency," and then find the "Send SOS message" option.
3. Finally, next to the "Send SOS messages" option, you should see a switch; turn it on. Then, when the SOS feature is turned on, choose which people you want to get the alert.
4. Pick a technique you want for starting the SOS message function; for example, you can set it to activate after three or four presses of the side button.
5. Choose one of the following choices to personalize what your phone will do when the SOS function is turned on:
    *   Select "Auto-call someone" if you want your phone to contact a specific number when you press the SOS button.
    *   When you choose this option, your phone can take images of the front and rear of your location and send them with your SOS message.

- If you'd rather have your phone record background noise for around five seconds before sending the SOS message, you can do so by selecting the "Add audio" option.

You can now activate the SOS message function by pushing the power button three or four times on your smartphone. This will trigger it to send an SOS message to all the contacts you have in your emergency contacts list. By taking this preventative step, you can be certain that your selected contacts will respond quickly and effectively in an emergency.

How to Deactivate Emergency SOS

If you want to disable the SOS function on your smartphone, or if you happen to have mistakenly turned it on and would like to turn it off, the following steps can be taken:

- In your device's Settings, locate the "Safety and emergency" area, and then tap on "Send SOS messages." Just toggle the button there to disable the SOS function.
- Additional security measures can be implemented to make the SOS button more difficult to accidentally press. Picture it as if you were to encrypt your SOS button. A higher threshold for sending the SOS message can be set. That way, you can set the SOS function to activate at a more deliberate time.

CHAPTER SIXTEEN
PHONE APP

How to make a call

A phone call can be made after the device is turned on and linked to a cellular network. It all begins on the main screen. The main shortcuts are a row of four or five icons down the screen's bottom, above the Device Function buttons (see the picture below for an illustration).

Your phone's main shortcuts may be somewhat different, but in this example, they are:

- Phone
- Camera
- Email
- Messages.

Here are the steps to make a call:

1. Press the Phone icon ⏣ on the Home screen.
- A screen similar to the one seen on the left in the photographs below is what you see.
2. Press the number you want to dial.

Below, you can see the picture of the Keypad screen (on the right) where the numbers you've input are shown. It attempts to identify the caller as you write.

TIP: In the US, while making a long-distance call, you don't have to prefix the area code with 1. Just dial the area code and the seven-digit number. The area code and the number 1 can also be included for local calls. However, remember to include the 1 if you're going abroad. Just be prepared for international roaming costs!

3. To make the call, tap the blue phone icon 📞 located at the screen's base.

The screen changes to the screen shown on the right in the image below. That is your opportunity to make sure you dialed the desired number. You should be able to hear either a busy signal or the other party's phone ringing within a few seconds. After that, it becomes as natural as any other phone call.

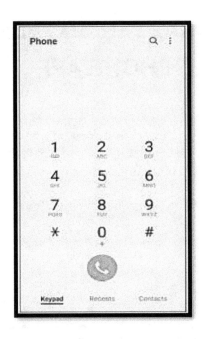

4. You can end your call by tapping the red phone button located on the screen's bottom.
- The line has been severed.

How to answer a call

It is much simpler to receive a call than to make one. You can see the caller's ID in a pop-up window whenever they phone you. You can see a few of the choices that pop up when you get a call in the picture below.

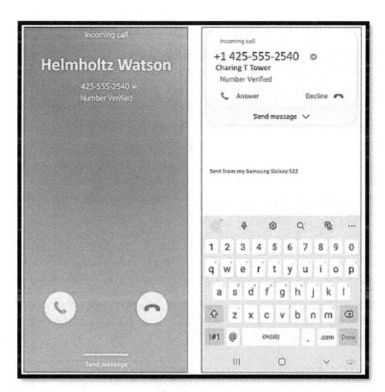

The whole screen (picture on the left above) will be shown if the phone is not currently doing anything. An app, like the one on the right, will display a pop-up screen while you're using it. The blue phone button can be pressed and dragged to answer calls. The pop-up screen to answer can appear at any time, even if you're in the middle of doing anything else on your phone, like music or playing a game. Until the call ends, you won't be able to play any media, including music or videos. Callers will need to set up your voicemail before they can leave you a message. A pre-recorded message will inform the caller that your voicemail account is not yet configured if you have not yet done so. When you activate your account and get your phone, certain cellular providers can set up voicemail for you; however, with other providers, you must do it yourself. Visit a carrier shop or go to the handbook that came with your phone to learn more about voicemail. Almost every mobile phone has the same answer/reject icons. But your Galaxy S24 isn't your average smartphone. Your specific phone determines the outcome of the third choice. On top of the usual answer/reject choices, you now have the option to reject the call and text the sender instead. Not only can you send a quick text message to the caller as they reach your voicemail, but you can also accept the call right away.

Here are a few examples of common premade messages:

- Sorry, I'm busy. Call back later.
- I'm in a meeting.
- I'll call you back.
- I'm at the movie theater.
- I'm in class.

To respond, just touch the appropriate message. You can let the person know that you're not ignoring them; you're simply unable to speak at the moment since the message is delivered as a text immediately. That finishing touch will be perfect. Something like "Please, just go away from me" or "I am too busy to talk to you right now" can be written and saved by you. Being courteous is another option. By using the "Compose new message" button, you can easily construct your very own pre-written message. You'll be able to access it later on your phone.

Just a friendly reminder: The phone number being called must have the capability to receive text messages. If the person phoning you is using a landline or another kind of mobile device that can't receive texts, this function won't activate.

How to decline and end a call

Ignoring the ringing is one option, but you can also stop a call by pressing and sliding the red button . Regardless of the situation, the call goes straight to voicemail and the ringing stops.

The recent call section

The ability to see a log of your call history is a great component of most mobile phones. While some landline phones may display the caller's identity, the vast majority of landline phones do not save the number of the person you contacted. Conversely, cell phones record every number you dialed. When you need to return a call but don't have the number on hand, this information can be very helpful. A number can also be quickly and simply added to a phone's contact list. You can see a log of all your calls, both incoming and outgoing, by tapping the Recents tab on your phone's screen.

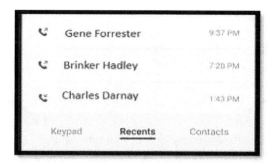

There is an icon that represents the following next to the call number:

- **Outgoing call you made:** An arrow pointing to the phone's silhouette, which indicates an outgoing call
- **Incoming call you received:** An arrow pointing away from the phone silhouette.
- **Incoming call you missed:** A bent arrow appears above the silhouette of the phone when there is an incoming call that you did not pick up.
- **Incoming call you ignored:** You declined a call that came in: A blue slash symbol next to the outline of the phone

You can easily find a contact's number or your own in the log, which keeps track of all the calls you've made and received. From the pop-up on the screen, you can do several things:

- To dial the number, touch the circle with the phone silhouette.
- Press the conversation bubble icon to text that number.
- If you are set up to make a video call, try making a video call.
- To save the number to your contact list, tap the symbol that appears in the call log (the i in the circle).

How to delete call records

- Launch the "Phone" app when you've found it.
- Just go to the "Recent" or "Call log" section. Your call logs will be seen here.
- Select the call(s) you want to remove by tapping and holding on to them. Multiple items can be selected by tapping on the checkboxes.
- Locate the "Delete" or "Trash" icon once you've chosen the call record(s). Toggle to that menu item.

How to block a number from calling you

1. **Navigate to the Phone Dialer:** First, find the phone dialer on your home screen and open it.
2. **Access Phone Settings:** Locate the three dots in the top right corner of Phone Settings.
3. **Open Settings Menu:** Go to the Settings menu by tapping the three dots. A little window will pop up on your phone, showing you a bunch of options.
4. **Select "Settings":** Go to the main menu and choose "Settings." A screen labeled "Call Settings" will then appear on your phone.
5. **Navigate to "Block Numbers":** Locate and pick the option labeled "Block Numbers" at the top of the list under the "Call Settings" page. Keep in mind that there could be other choices, including the ability to put a number on a "blacklist," that you can access.
6. **Select Blocking Method:** One option will be to add a contact after selecting "Block Numbers," while the other is to block an unknown caller.
7. **Block a Specific Contact:** Simply input the contact's phone number into the given box if you want to block them.
8. **Select Source:** From the Source menu, choose "Recent" or "Contacts." While selecting "Contacts" lets you import numbers from your existing contact list, selecting "Recent" means including just the numbers with whom you have recently communicated.
9. **Enter Phone Number:** Enter the phone number you want to block. The contact will then be added to your block list when you click the (+) icon.

How to Unblock Contact Numbers

These methods can be used to unblock numbers that were previously blocked. Select the desired contact number and click the red exclamation point to remove it from the list.

The way to accomplish it is this:

1. **Access the Block List:** Currently banned numbers can be seen in your phone's block list.
2. **Select Number to Unblock:** Find the number you want to unblock and click on it. If you want to resume receiving calls and texts, that is the number to unblock.
3. **Initiate Unblock Action:** On most contacts, you'll see a negative symbol (-) at the very end. To start unblocking, tap the minus symbol.
4. **Confirm Unblocking:** When asked, confirm that you want to unblock the number. At this point, you should be sure you want to unblock the chosen contact.
5. **Number Removal:** After you make a selection, the number will be immediately removed from the block list. It seems that you have unblocked the contact.
6. **Receiving Calls and Messages:** After the number is removed from the block list, you will no longer have any limitations on receiving calls and messages from that particular contact.

CHAPTER SEVENTEEN
SAMSUNG SETTINGS

How to activate the Do Not Disturb feature

You can silence notifications and background sounds by activating this mode. In addition to scheduling routine events like sleep or meetings, you can also make exceptions for specific people, apps, and alarms. You can access it by tapping the Settings button after entering the Quick Settings panel with a downward swipe on the screen. Change the setting for Notifications and Turn Off Notifications. You can customize the following settings: Do not disturb, for how long, sleeping, Add schedule, calls, texts, chats, alarms, sounds, applications, and hide notifications.

How to use Dark mode

1. Take a look at the **Display** section after opening the **Settings** app.
2. You'll see the **"Light"** and **"Dark"** options in the upper part of the screen. To activate the dark mode function, just click on the toggle button that appears next to the selection.
3. You can create a timetable under the Dark mode settings if you want not to have your smartphone always on dark mode. **"Sunrise to Sunset"** and **"Custom Schedule"** are the choices that will be shown to you.
   - If you would want the functionality to automatically turn on at night and turn off in the morning, choose the Sunrise to Sunset option.
   - To manually select the time when you want the functionality to be active and disabled, use the custom option.

As the light level in the room changes, the screen brightness of the Samsung Galaxy S24, S24+, and Ultra will adjust automatically. Your smartphone's screen brightness will be automatically dimmed while you're using it in low light. Your phone's screen brightness will be automatically adjusted to compensate for light environments. However, the automatic brightness adjustments on the S24, S24+, or S24 Ultra might be very harsh at times, making the screen seem too black or too light for your liking.

To find out how to resolve this issue:

1. Go to your Samsung Galaxy S24, S24+, or S24 Ultra and make sure that the Adaptive Brightness feature is off.

Here are the things you need to perform before you can achieve that:

- Open the **Settings** app on your phone.
- Choose **"Display"** from the main menu.
- Verify that the Adaptive Brightness option is active.

You can no longer boost the screen brightness using the Extra Brightness option after selecting Adaptive Brightness. Adaptive Brightness is a machine learning feature that, if enabled, allows your Samsung phone to gradually learn your preferred screen brightness.

2. Changing the screen brightness of your Galaxy S24, S24+, or S24 Ultra manually in different lighting conditions can help the automatic brightness feature work more accurately.

To access the Notification Panel, swipe down from the top of the screen. From there, you can manually adjust settings using the Quick Settings menu. Next, swipe the Notification Panel down to see the Quick Settings option. You can change the brightness using the bar that appears at the bottom of the page. Press the three-dot icon to bring up the Quick Settings menu, where you should see the brightness adjustment bar. After that, choose **Brightness Control** from the **Quick Panel Layout** menu. Lastly, under the Brightness Control menu, choose Always Show. Going to the Display option in the Settings app is another way to adjust the brightness. Keep adjusting the screen brightness until it's exactly perfect. Over time, the Adaptive Brightness feature will pick up on your tastes and adjust the brightness more precisely.

3. You could be obstructing the light sensor on your Samsung Galaxy S24, S24+, or S24 Ultra if the auto-brightness problem persists.

Located just below the front camera, this sensor is ideal for use while holding your phone in portrait mode. To the right of the front camera, when held in landscape position, is where you'll find the light sensor on a smartphone.

How to adjust screen brightness

1. Start by navigating to the Settings menu. Click on Display.

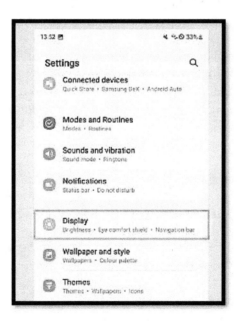

2. Modify settings for the display

Peruse the available choices and adjust the display settings using the corresponding sliders and toggles. What follows is a walkthrough of all of these options.

3. **Use the brightness slider**

To adjust the level of brightness on your screen, you can locate the brightness slider in the main Display menu. Toggle adaptive brightness to have your phone adapt to the light level in your immediate vicinity. You can utilize Extra brightness if you keep this option off; however, it quickly drains the battery but raises the maximum brightness you can use.

Select Adaptive or Standard Motion smoothness

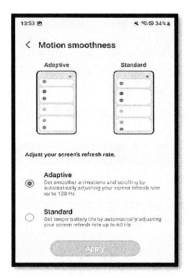

How smoothly your screen refreshes is affected by motion smoothness. After selecting one, touch the Apply button. While adaptive allows the display to shift from 1Hz up to 120Hz, standard locks it at 60Hz to save power but makes the performance less smooth.

Use the Eye comfort shield settings

To help you get a better night's rest by lowering the amount of blue light produced by your screen, Eye Comfort Shield allows you to adjust the color temperature of your display. From this menu, you can choose an automated adjustment option, create a personalized timetable, or activate an enhanced comfort mode that modifies the display's color profile even further.

Screen mode settings

You can adjust the way your phone shows colors by switching to screen mode. You can adjust the saturation level of the color scheme using the two preset options, Vivid and Natural. Under the Advanced Settings menu, you can create a personalized RGB mix, and in Vivid mode, you can change the display's white balance.

How to change font style

1. **Access the Apps Drawer:** To access the drawer that houses all of your programs, swipe up from the bottom of your screen.
2. **Open Settings:** Go to the Apps drawer and select the Settings icon to open the Settings app. From there, you can access all the setup choices.
3. **Navigate to Display Settings:** Look for "Display" in the options app and touch on it to access the display-related options for your phone.

4. **Adjust Font Size and Style:** Change the font's size and style by tapping the "Font Size and Style" option that appears as you scroll down.
5. **Change Font Style:** To switch up the font style, just tap on the one you're using now. Doing so will bring up a font style preview from which you can choose a new one for your device.
6. **Explore Different Fonts:** You can see what other possibilities are available and choose the one that you like most by touching on different font types.
7. **Download New Fonts:** To add more fonts to your library, choose "Download Fonts." Before you go to the Galaxy Shop to download fonts, make sure your internet connection is functioning.
8. **Download and Apply a Font:** After you've found one you like, just hit the "Download" button. Just a moment or two will pass while the download is underway.
9. **View Newly Downloaded Font:** To see the font you just downloaded, go back to the font settings page by using the back button. The typeface you just downloaded should now be shown in the list.
10. **Enable the New Font:** To activate the font you downloaded, tap on it. By doing so, you will return to the previous page where you made your preferences.
11. **Adjust Font Size:** Change the font size to your preference by dragging the slider to the right to enlarge and to the left to shrink it on the preferences screen.

Additionally:

- Activate Bold font for more contrast between text and background.
- Enable the high-contrast keyboard if you have difficulty seeing letters when typing.

Note: Please be aware that there is no dedicated selection for high-contrast fonts. A wider variety of typefaces can be available to you in the future, however, if you download more from the Galaxy store.

How to use a screensaver

After your Galaxy phone or tablet's screen goes down automatically while charging, presenting a screensaver. **Here you can find instructions on how to install a screensaver on a Samsung smartphone.**

1. Navigate to the **Display** menu in your **Settings**.
2. From the option that appears, choose Screensaver.
3. Pick a Screensaver you Love.
4. After selecting Photo Frame, Photo Table, or Photos, touch the settings.
5. Set an album as the screensaver.
6. After your phone screen goes off, you can see the screensaver photos you've selected as your background while it charges.

How to activate Find My Mobile

Find My Mobile is a free service offered by Samsung that allows users to locate, back up, and remove data from a registered Galaxy mobile device by using their Samsung account. You can monitor the location of your smartphone even when it is switched off thanks to the Find My Mobile feature. In addition, you can prohibit access to Samsung Pay, backup your data to Samsung Cloud, and even manage your device remotely using the Find My Mobile website. Use the 'Find My Mobile' tool to find your smartphone, lock it, and create a backup of it.

If you want to find your phone, you can use the "Find My Mobile" option.

1. Your Samsung account has to be configured on the device you are using.
2. You consent to the terms and conditions of using wireless networks and give Google permission to collect information about your location with your consent.
- **Find my device**: Accessibility differs depending on the mobile device and/or operating system.
- **Data backup**: For data backup, if your device is not connected to a Wi-Fi network, it will connect to your mobile network. Depending on the payment plan that you have, this can result in additional fees.

Activating Find My Phone

- On your Galaxy smartphone, go to the **Settings** menu and choose **"Biometrics and security."**
- From that location, choose the **"Find My Mobile"** option and toggle it. To log in, you will need to use the information associated with your Samsung account, or you can establish a new account if you do not already have one.
- At that point, you will be presented with the opportunity to activate several different choices, including **"Remote unlock"** and **"Send the last location."**
- Take note that in the Settings section of your mobile operator, the Google Find My Device service can be offered in place of Samsung Find My Cell. Find My Device will be how you will establish a connection to your Google account. Both of these programs provide access to a significant number of the same features.

Locating a Phone using Find My Mobile

After you have activated the Find My Mobile service, you can use any web browser to locate your Samsung mobile device while utilizing the service. You will be required to re-enter your login information for your Samsung account. Once this is complete, you will be shown a list of all Samsung devices for which Find My Mobile has been activated. If your device is identified, the location of your device will be shown on the map. In addition to this, you will be able to see the current status of the device, including the battery life and the network connection. The location tracking and other functionalities of Find My Mobile will only operate if your smartphone is turned on and connected to a cellular or Wi-Fi network. It is important to keep this in mind. If you want to give yourself the best possible opportunity to discover your device, you should log in as soon as you become aware that it has been lost.

What happens if my battery runs out?

If the battery has already died, Find My Mobile will be unable to establish the current location of your handset. If you had activated the **"Send the last location"** feature on your smartphone, it ought to have automatically notified its position to the Find My Mobile service once the battery level went below 20%. This can help retrieve the device so long as it is not moving about at the time being recovered.

Lock the screen, prevent the phone from turning off, and display a contact message

Find My Mobile gives you the ability to lock your smartphone remotely if you are concerned that it has been unlocked. You can also prevent other individuals from turning off the device, which will enable you to track its whereabouts. On the screen, you can also show a contact message and your phone number, making it possible for anybody who discovers the gadget to get in touch with you.

Managing a Device on the Move

If you believe your device is moving, choose the **"Track position"** option. When that time has passed, you will be able to get an automated update on its whereabouts every fifteen minutes.

Backing Up Data or Deleting a Lost Device

You can try doing a remote backup of your data if you are unable to locate the device that you have misplaced. To utilize this service, you will need to ensure that Samsung Cloud is activated on your mobile device. It is possible to back up a significant amount of data to Samsung Cloud and retrieve it if you get a new smartphone. By pressing the "erase" button, you can also utilize Find My Mobile to remotely delete all of the data on your device and do a factory reset. Remember that doing this will also destroy your Samsung account from the device that you have lost, making it hard to find it again. This is something you should bear in mind before you proceed.

Prolonging a Lost Device's Battery

Find My Mobile also allows you to remotely change the power-saving settings of your phone, which can help you extend the battery life of your phone that has gone missing. Adjust the battery-saving mode on your smartphone to its maximum setting to increase the amount of time it remains on so that you can locate it.

Accessing a Locked Device

Find My Mobile can be helpful even if you did not misplace your mobile device, such as a phone or tablet. Instead of using the Personal Identification Number (PIN) or password to unlock your smartphone, you can use the Find My Mobile feature to locate it. You must choose "Remote Unlock" throughout the process of registering your device if you want to make use of this capability. You should take every care to protect yourself from potential security risks, such as the loss of data or theft if you lose your device. To our great relief, the Find My Phone function makes this process quite easy. This feature gives you the best possible opportunity to reunite with your lost smartphone by tracking its location, preventing the device from turning off, and extending the amount of time the battery can last. If the phone is found by an unintended stranger, they will get a message that contains your contact details.

CHAPTER EIGHTEEN
SAMSUNG FUNCTIONS

How to use Samsung Pay

To begin the procedure, you must first ensure that your Galaxy S24 is equipped with Samsung Pay. Although this software is quite amazing, there are a lot of advantages to using this technology, and your carrier would have liked not to have it installed.

Detailed information about the app page can be found below. If you choose Install, you will see the picture that is located on the right.

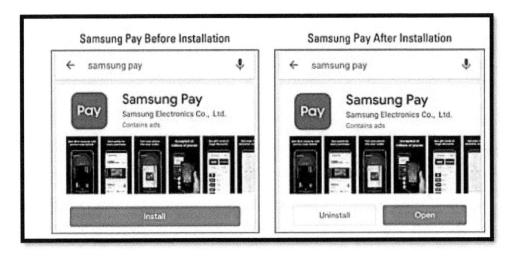

The Samsung Pay app operates in a manner that sets it apart from the majority of other applications. Whenever you use Samsung Pay for the first time, you will be provided with instructions on how to use it, asked to enter your credit card information (in a manner that is quite handy, by the way), and asked to consent to a variety of permissions and agreements. After you have provided all of this information, Samsung Pay will be waiting eagerly at the bottom of your home pages, ready to fulfill your payment requirements with nothing more than a simple swipe from the bottom of the screen. To put it simply, the vast majority of individuals would not utilize this application if they were required to search through their displays to locate it. In this manner, you will not be required to look for the application and wait for it to appear on the screen.

Setting Up Samsung Pay

When you launch the Samsung Pay application, you will be presented with several pages right up to the point when you reach the Home screen. These pages consist of marketing introductions, permissions and agreements (which you are required to grant to proceed), and a few pages that validate that Samsung Pay can be used on your phone.

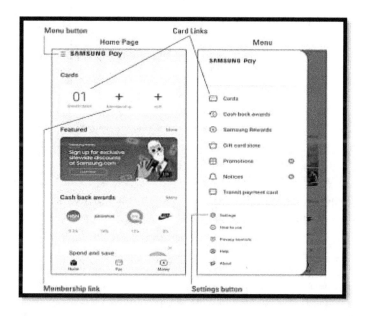

Both the fact that you are in one of the 29 countries where Samsung Pay is accepted and the fact that your phone has the appropriate components (which will be the case for your Galaxy S24, but this is not the case for every Android phone) are things that the application needs to verify. Whether you are in the United States of America, Canada, China, or Kazakhstan (which is extremely wonderful!), you are all set. The situation is hopeless if you are, for example, in Yemen. If you are not located in one of these countries, Samsung may not have all of the necessary arrangements in place for you to use this app. This is because each nation has its legislation regarding payments, and Samsung may not have all of the necessary arrangements in place. In the shortest amount of time feasible, more nations will be included. The next stage in the first setup procedure is to go through the process of setting up the security in the manner that you wish. During the process of conducting a transaction, you have the choice of either using your fingerprint or providing a personal identification number (PIN).

In some circumstances, it could be more convenient to use a Samsung Pay personal identification number (PIN) rather than a fingerprint. When it comes to most situations, using your fingerprint is a very handy option. If you have not yet taken the necessary steps to set them up, the Samsung

Pay app will guide you through the process. It is effortless and fast. The next thing you need to do is input the information for your credit card. If you go to the main page or the menu and press the link that reads Cards, you will be directed to a screen that displays the photos of the credit cards that you have added to your account. An empty screen will be shown at the beginning. You can see what it looks like once you have inserted your first card in the picture that is provided below.

Tap the blue circle in the lower-right corner of the screen that has a silhouette of a credit card and a plus symbol on it. This will allow you to add a new card. You will see a pop-up window with a few options. Choosing the option to Add a Credit/Debit Card will get you started with this procedure. The picture on the left represents the moment when the screen initially appears, and the image on the right represents the moment when the credit card of your choice is shown in the viewfinder.

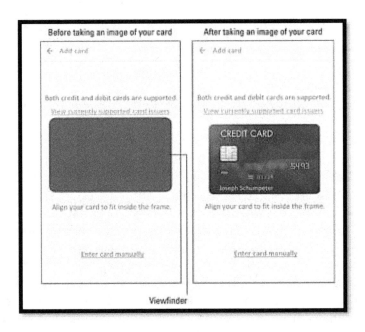

The information that is printed on the face of your credit card is subsequently interpreted by the application, which then populates as many displays as it can with the information contained on your credit card. If it can't figure out the information on your card or if the information is on the back of the card, it will ask you to fill out a form. By selecting the Next button, Samsung Pay will make an effort to verify the information with your credit card provider. Doing so will not incur any expenses for you. If you do decide to make a charge, it just wants to ensure that everything will go without any problems. The corporation will want to make sure that you are permitted to use that credit card is one of the things that they will want to check. This indicates that you must either be the principal cardholder or you must coordinate with the person who has the primary card. It is important to keep in mind that the legal ramifications of scanning your fingerprint and touching your phone on a credit card reader are identical to those of actually signing a credit slip. An acknowledgment is sent to you after the credit card company has confirmed that everything is in order and appropriate order.

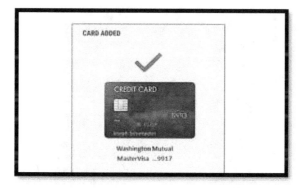

How to Make Use of Samsung Pay

To begin, choose an item to purchase from a store. Inform the cashier that you will be paying with a credit card and have them ring it up for you. Make a swipe upward on the screen.

Simply tapping the symbol, you can enter your fingerprint. You should either hold your phone against the location where the magnetic stripe would be read by the credit card reader or it should be held against the location where the contactless payment system logo is located, if it is accessible. This is shown in the picture below. This will cause the semicircle that is located above your signature to begin counting down, and your phone will vibrate to let you know that it is transmitting. You will be able to hear a beep if everything is successful. If it does not work for whatever reason, you can try again by just inputting your security choice the second time. **Tip**: It is important to note that this method is compatible with the great majority of credit card readers. On the other hand, this does not work very well with credit card readers, particularly those that require you to place your card into the machine and then rapidly remove it. Most of the time, this particular kind of reader is seen at petrol stations. There is a growing number of gas stations that are equipped with a contactless reader; nevertheless, there are several generations of gas stations available, so your mileage may vary.

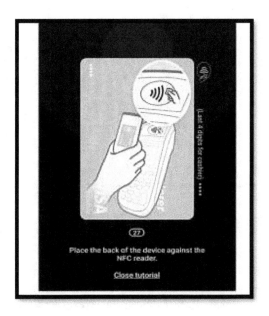

Using Gift Cards with Samsung Pay

Adding an Existing Gift Card

Gift cards that have been bought other than via Samsung Pay can be added to your account. Start Samsung Pay by clicking the three horizontal lines that appear, selecting Menu, and then selecting Cards from the list of options. To load gift cards, pick the Gift tab, and then select the symbol that looks like a gift card. Investigate the store that is included on the list, and choose them. Click the Confirm button after you have entered the Card number and PIN. Your gift card will be successfully added to your Samsung Pay account. Pressing the OK button will complete the process.

Checking Gift Card Balance

When you use Samsung Pay, the balance on your gift card will often be shown. On the other hand, certain merchants deliberately opt not to disclose this information. To see the remaining balance on your gift cards, open Samsung Pay, click Menu (the three horizontal lines), and then pick Cards from the menu that appears. Following the selection of the Gift option, choose the card that you would want to see. The gift card balance will be shown on the information page of the card. To bring the balance up to date, tap the Refresh sign.

Managing Samsung Pay

This application is largely self-sufficient so long as you continue to pay your credit card payments and maintain your credit card account with the bank. Despite this, you will sometimes be required to visit the settings of the application. Simply touching the Samsung Pay logo that appears on the app screen will take you there. The Add link should be tapped to add a new credit or debit card. The addition of a second card is simple, and the photos will be stacked on top of each other when they are shown on this page. The rapid launch link will bring up the card that is currently at the top of the list. If you would want to switch to using a different credit card, you can go through the available alternatives available to you. Not only can Samsung Pay accept credit and debit cards, but it is also delighted to assist you with membership cards and loyalty cards. Avoid being timid. Experiment with it and see whether you like the ease it provides. Tap the three dots to bring up a pop-up menu for the Samsung Pay settings, and then pick Settings from the menu that appears.

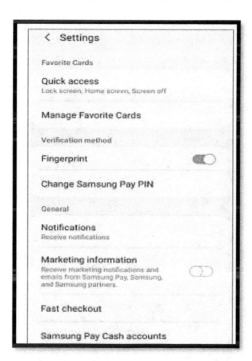

To remove a credit card or modify its settings, all you need to do is tap on the link that says Manage Favorite Cards. This will allow you to do any of these things. Each piece of information that is connected to that card will be shown on the screen.

SAMSUNG DEX

Through the use of Samsung DeX, which is a creative solution, it is possible to convert your phone into a powerful laptop or desktop computer in a very easy manner. To get the most out of your experience, you can even connect a keyboard and mouse to your phone, leaving your laptop at home (or in its bag) for the ultimate experience.

Connect your device and launch Samsung DeX

Through the use of an HDMI adapter, the Samsung DeX can be used most conveniently by connecting your phone to a television or monitor. It is recommended that you use the uni USB-C to HDMI cable that is given below; however, any HDMI to USB-C wire should work just fine.

Please take your cable and follow the instructions that are stated below.

1. To access your quick toggles, you must first double-click the status bar.
2. When you see the DeX button, scroll over to it and tap it.
3. If you do not see the DeX option, open your system settings, choose Connected Devices, and then select Samsung Dex.
4. The HDMI end of the USB-C cable should be connected to your television or monitor, and the USB-C end should be connected to your phone if DeX has been engaged.
5. A desktop user interface ought to appear on your screen in a short amount of time.

As soon as this user interface appears, the screen of your Galaxy phone will transform into a touchpad. The on-screen cursor can be controlled using this, much like a trackpad on a laptop system.

How to use the Samsung Health App

The Samsung Health app is a piece of fitness software that, as its name indicates, enables you to monitor a wide range of fitness statistics while simultaneously encouraging you to develop healthy habits. If you have an iOS device, you can get the program by downloading it from the Google Play Store, the Galaxy Store, or the App Store. It is not necessary to have a Samsung wristwatch to make use of the application since you can track fundamental metrics such as the number of steps, walks and runs using your phone. Synchronizing a smartwatch, on the other hand, will provide you with the most comprehensive experience that is conceivable.

At the same time, the user interface and the general design of the application are both simple. You will find all of the relevant information presented to you on the home page in the shape of rectangular cards. This will make it easy for you to analyze your progress toward attaining your goals at a glance. On the Together page, you can create pleasant competitions with your friends and family, although the Fitness tab is where you will discover training plans and other material related to fitness.

Tracking Health Metrics with Samsung Health

By using the accelerometer that is included in your smartphone, Samsung Health can monitor essentials such as the number of steps you take, the number of calories you consume, the number of walks you take, the number of runs you do, and total activity.

A complete breakdown of all of the health and fitness measurements that are accessible with Samsung Health is provided in the following paragraphs.

1. **Daily Activity:** The first area is titled "Daily Activity," and it is where customers can acquire a thorough description of their daily physical activities. A comprehensive summary of physical activity participation is included, as well as essential metrics such as the total number of steps taken, the total distance traveled, the number of calories burned, and the total number of steps taken.
2. **Heart Rate:** This section provides consumers with sophisticated information regarding the state of their cardiovascular health. Not only does it reveal the average resting heart rate, but it also outlines the dynamic range of heart rate. This is accomplished by drawing on data obtained from the wearable device that the user is using, which can be a band or a wristwatch.
3. **Exercise:** The third component is exercise, which goes beyond simple activity monitoring by providing a comprehensive analysis of a wide range of different types of physical workouts. To give a full evaluation of an individual's fitness routine, it offers specific information on heart rate zones, the length of time spent working out, the amount of calories burned, and other parameters.

4. **Sleep:** If it is engaged, the Sleep function provides the user with a comprehensive examination of their nocturnal behaviors. This includes a careful analysis of the amount of time spent in each of the four stages of sleep, the monitoring of blood oxygen levels, and even the incorporation of snoring detection for a more comprehensive knowledge of the quality of sleep.

5. **Body Composition:** This feature, which delves into the complexities of body composition, exposes the proportionate distribution of essential components based on total body weight. These components include fat, skeletal muscle, and water. However, to do this, you will need to make use of more powerful gadgets such as the Galaxy Watch 5 or Galaxy Watch 4, or a smart scale that provides compatibility.

6. **Stress:** The Stress function is responsible for doing a full examination of an individual's stress levels. This evaluation is carried out by using biomarkers such as heart rate. Additionally, it incorporates guided deep breathing exercises as a useful tool for stress management and relaxation at the same time.

7. **Blood Oxygen:** This function allows users to manually record readings or choose for automatic operation while they are sleeping, which provides a detailed knowledge of oxygen levels in the bloodstream. It does this by measuring the proportion of hemoglobin that is contained inside oxygenated red blood cells.

8. **Blood Pressure:** The Blood Pressure function provides users with insights into their blood pressure readings by drawing upon data from either a Galaxy Watch 4/5 or a compatible blood pressure monitoring device. This helps users develop a more comprehensive perception of their overall health.

9. **Food and Water:** This feature gives users the ability to manually record their food and water consumption, which enables them to get a more in-depth knowledge of their dietary patterns. It also provides a tailored approach to nutrition.

10. **Blood Glucose:** The Blood Glucose feature incorporates data from a glucose meter that is compatible with the application. This feature gives users real-time information about their current blood glucose levels, which improves both awareness and control of glucose levels.

11. **Women's Health:** Designed exclusively for female users, the Women's Health feature makes it possible to meticulously follow the menstrual cycle and the menstruation schedule. This helps to promote a more educated and tailored approach to reproductive health practices.

Exploring Additional Features in Samsung Health

When you participate in the Together program that Samsung Health provides, you will be able to include some friendly rivalry into the process of accomplishing your fitness goals. Using the Together option, you and your friends and family can compete against one another to see who can walk the most steps for a week or a month, or who can attain a given step count first. You can even see who can walk the most steps in a certain amount of time. The purpose of this is not only to keep you motivated but also to help your friends and family stay on track toward the fulfillment of their fitness goals in a consistent manner for themselves. In addition, you can invite other people to take part in the challenges with you, which will transform the activity into one that is not just competitive but also entertaining.

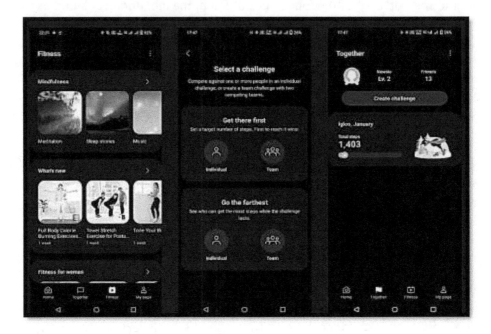

In addition to enabling you to monitor your physical activity, the Fitness part of Samsung Health offers a curated collection of information that is relevant to health. This content includes a range of personalized exercises, calming music, sleep tales, and guided meditations, among other things. This particular area can be found inside the Samsung Health app. This is a wonderful place to start if you are starting in the realm of fitness for the first time. Because there is such a broad range of training regimens accessible, it will not be difficult for you to find one that matches your specific fitness target. This is true regardless of whether your purpose is to increase the amount of muscle mass you have or to have a more toned look. You will always be aware of what to do since each workout comes with both a video instruction that is easy to comprehend and an audio guide that will help you through the process. This option allows you to rapidly access your fitness routines, and it also allows you to download them so that you can use them even when you are not connected to the internet.

How to use the Samsung Notes App

Taking a lot of notes on your phone can cause Samsung Notes to get crowded, so use caution. You should not be concerned about this since it comes equipped with features that will make it much easier for you to manage your notes. For example, you can make it simpler to explore by splitting your notes into the many categories that are accessible to you. As an alternative to browsing through each of your notes one at a time, you now have the option of searching for notes that include certain names or topics.

This is a list of some of the most useful features that are incorporated in Samsung Notes, and they are as follows:

- **Quick highlight:** This function enables you to choose an action of your choice and highlight a portion of the text in a very short time. When you touch and hold a word with your S Pen, you can highlight more text by dragging it across the screen to highlight further text. This is how you can highlight additional text. You will be presented with several alternatives to choose from, such as the ability to cut, copy, paste, display the clipboard, display the dictionary, and share an image.
- **Zoom in and out:** To zoom in or out, just pinch the screen for the desired effect.
- **The search function:** Make use of this tool to search for and discover the particular note that you are looking for. The next step is to choose the Search option from the toolbar, and then manually enter the phrases that you are looking for.
- **Organize your notes:** There are many different choices available to you from which you can choose to organize your notes. Proceed to pick Edit from the menu that displays after you have selected Additional options, which are represented by three vertical dots. Decide which of the available options you would want to proceed with, and then choose the notes that you want to use. You have the choice of hitting Move to move the files to a new folder, touching Share to send the files to another place, or tapping Delete to delete the files from your phone. All of these options are available to you.
- **Lock your notes**: If you want to make sure that some notes, like your poetry collection, are kept a secret, you can set a lock on your notes. After launching the note you want to use, go to the Additional Options menu (which is represented by three vertical dots), and then pick the Lock icon from the list of alternatives that appears. In the next step, you will be required to create a password for your note by following the instructions that appear on the screen.

Note: If you wish to change the password, go to the settings menu on your Samsung Notes device, pick the **"Note unlock methods"** option, and then select the **"Change password"** option. This will allow you to change the password. You are going to require a Samsung account to keep your notes safe.

- **Sort your notes**: Arrange your notes in the following order: Because you have so many notes, you are completely clueless about what any of them are. The process of sorting them can be of assistance to you in determining what is going on. Tap the Filter button that is situated on the home screen of the Samsung Notes application, and then choose the choice that you like to use, such as "Date generated." Now you are ready to use the Filter feature. The format of your notes can also be changed in its entirety, which is another choice available to you. Simply click the Additional Choices button, which appears to be three vertical dots, and then pick View from the menu that appears after that. This will allow you to customize the way the notes are presented.

- **Action icons**: If you make use of this feature, your handwritten notes will be accompanied by icons. Simply pressing on the different icons enables you to do tasks like making phone calls, sending emails, solving equations, and going straight to websites from the icons themselves. In the top left corner of the screen, you will see a button that looks like three horizontal lines. Touch this button, then hit the icon that represents Settings, and last, press the switch that is located next to the icons that represent Action.

How to Save Notes

You can back up and synchronize your notes with Samsung Notes using the following options:

Synchronize with Samsung Account: If you want your notes to be synced across all of the devices linked to your Samsung account and kept automatically in Samsung Notes, you can enable synchronization by opting in. The result is a streamlined and consistent method of taking notes.
Back-Up Using File Choices: To save a copy of your notes, check out Samsung Notes' several file options. You can choose the file format that works best for you, giving you the freedom to keep your notes safely in a way that fits you.
Utilize Samsung Cloud: If you own several Galaxy smartphones, you can use Samsung Cloud to keep your notes in sync. With this function, you can access your notes from anywhere, providing a seamless environment for all of your note-taking requirements. You can make all of your notes in one place, sync them with Samsung Cloud, and then access them from any of your Galaxy devices with ease.

1. To access the settings, open the **Samsung Notes** app. Then, tap the **menu** icon, which appears as three horizontal lines then select the settings icon.
2. Select **Sync with Samsung account** from the menu once you've enabled the rights.
3. Press the toggle at the page's top to enable or disable the feature. Another alternative is to press the Sync Notes data button, where you can choose how your notes will be synced. Both Wi-Fi and mobile data can be used to synchronize your notes.
4. If you want to save your notes in a different format, you can do so in several ways. There are several other file formats from which you can choose to save it: text, images, PDF, Word, and PowerPoint. Following the selection of the desired note (represented by the three vertical dots), tap the **More Options** icon to access further backup options. Then, use the Save as File option to choose the file type you want to save.

How to Import/Export Data

Perhaps Samsung Notes isn't displaying your Google Drive notes. You can rest easy knowing that importing them to your phone is a breeze, and then they will show up on the app. To import data into Samsung Notes, open the app, then press the Menu sign (which looks like three horizontal lines). Then, touch the Settings button. Choose the option to import your notes. Just follow the on-screen prompts after tapping the source you want to import from, such as your Samsung account. One other thing you can do with Samsung Notes is import and export PDF files. The program will let you annotate and sketch on the Documents, but you won't have any editing capabilities.

How to Update Samsung Notes

Keep Samsung Notes updated at all times in case more note-taking features are released. Press the Menu button (three horizontal lines) to access the app's settings. Then, hit the Settings icon. To check for available updates, go to About Samsung Notes and then tap Update. By enabling automatic updates from the Galaxy Store and the Google Play Store, you can keep your Samsung Notes running the latest software version at all times.

Managing Note Styles, Templates, and Folders

To quickly locate the information you need from your Samsung Notes notebooks, it is recommended to keep them in an organized manner. You can arrange and display your notes in a variety of ways using the tools provided by the program. If you want your notes to be uniform, put all of the pertinent ones in one folder or use a template.

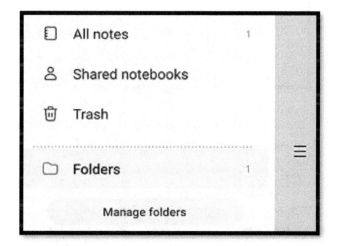

How to Share Notes

Has Samsung Notes ever been used for doodling a cute picture or writing down meeting details? Numerous file formats are available for internal application sharing, so you can easily email it to yourself, a friend, or a coworker.

As an example, you might email yourself a Word document or PDF file with the work notes!

1. Start up the Samsung Notes app. Then, choose the note you want to edit. Finally, tap the More Options icon and you'll see three vertical dots.

2. After you touch the Share button, choose the kind of file you want to share. Depending on your needs, you can choose between many file formats, including Samsung Notes, PDF, Word, PowerPoint, Pictures, and Text.

3. After you've decided on the file type, you can choose the sharing method, such as sending an email or a text message, among others. Choose an option that suits you best for sending the file.

Keep in mind that not all common file formats can be exchanged in all common ways. Before you choose a file-sharing mechanism, be sure it works with the kind of file you have.

How to use Voice typing

Two voice-to-text apps—one from Google and one from Samsung—are preinstalled on your Galaxy S24. Any of these voice typing capabilities can be activated by following these steps:

1. Launch your device's **Settings** app.
2. Find the **"General management"** area and go to the **"Keyboard list and default"** option. Samsung Voice Input can be activated by toggling the switch that is shown next to it.
3. For one voice assistant feature to work on your smartphone, you must also deactivate the others.
4. You can now text messages with the aid of the voice assistant. Go ahead and give the messaging app a go.
5. Say what you want to type into the microphone by long-pressing the icon on the keyboard's toolbar.
6. Lower your hand from the symbol after you have finished speaking.

CHAPTER NINETEEN
CONNECTION ON GALAXY S24

Bluetooth

1. **Access Settings:** Open Settings by tapping the Settings icon on your Home screen.
2. **Navigate to Bluetooth Settings:** To access Bluetooth in the Settings app, go to "Connections," and then tap on, "Bluetooth."
- Please be aware that the following instructions are based on the assumption that you are using a software version of the Galaxy S24, Galaxy S24+, or Galaxy S24 that has these capabilities. Additionally, the exact layout can differ somewhat depending on upgrades.
3. **Enable/Disable Bluetooth:** You can turn Bluetooth on and off using the settings screen for Bluetooth. You can do this by tapping the gear icon in the upper right corner of your screen.
- Other devices can find and pair with your smartphone if you enable Bluetooth.

How to unpair from a Bluetooth device

- Locate the "Connections" option in the Settings menu and touch on it. This is where you can adjust your device's Bluetooth and other connection settings.
- To access Bluetooth, go to the Connections menu and choose it. You can manage your connected devices under the Bluetooth settings, which this will take you to.
- A list of devices that are currently linked will appear when you access the Bluetooth settings. Use the list to locate the device that you want to unpair.
- An information symbol (often an 'i' in a circle) or three vertical dots can be located next to the Bluetooth device that you want to unpair. Device options can be accessed by tapping this symbol or the three dots.
- To disconnect your device, go to its settings and search for an option that says "**Unpair**," "**Forget**," or "**Disconnect**." The specific language could change based on the model and version of your operating system. To begin the process of unpairing, tap on this option.
- If you're not sure you want to disconnect the device, a confirmation window may pop up. Choose "Unpair" or an equivalent option to confirm the action.
- To unpair a device, first make sure it is no longer shown in the list of paired devices. The unpairing procedure was successful, as confirmed by this.

How to set up the Internet on your device

- Beginning at the top of the screen, slide two fingers downwards.
- Tap the settings icon.
- Tap Connections.

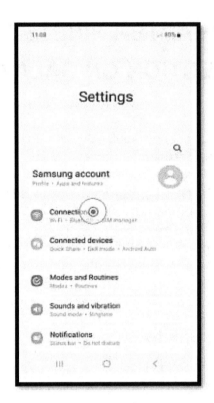

- Tap Mobile networks.

- Tap Access Point Names
- To add, tap on the Add button.

- Your network provider's name and APN must be entered. Their website or other means of communication can provide you with this data.

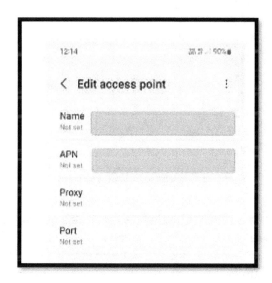

- Select "Save" from the menu that appears after tapping the Menu button.

- APNs can be easily added and selected by tapping the radio button next to them.
- Give your phone a restart.

How to use Wi-Fi Calling

If there is no signal, then it does not matter. No worries there, thanks to Wi-Fi Calling from compatible providers. In areas without cell service, you can still utilize this feature to communicate over Wi-Fi. Poor signal won't ever be an excuse to turn you down again. Please be aware that not all service providers or devices support Wi-Fi Calling.

Enable Wi-Fi Calling

There will be no more aimless meandering while we seek a signal. You can use your phone's network connection to make calls when Wi-Fi Calling is turned on. For this feature to work, your phone has to be linked to a Wi-Fi network and have an active SIM card.

1. Begin by opening the **Phone app**.
2. After you touch **More options** (the three vertical dots), pick **Settings**.
3. Press the switch, and then choose Wi-Fi Calling, to enable the feature. Click **Save** after reviewing and entering your emergency contact information if prompted to do so by a popup.
4. You can now make calls via Wi-Fi. To disable Wi-Fi Calling, just click the button one more.
5. On certain phones, you can find the option to activate Wi-Fi calling under the Quick settings menu. To enable Wi-Fi Calling, use two fingers to swipe down from the top of the screen, and then tap the symbol.

After that, users can update their emergency details by visiting Wi-Fi Calling and selecting either Update existing emergency address or Emergency Location Information.

Wi-Fi Calling Preferences

- Carriers can have different alternatives available to you. If your Wi-Fi or cellular network goes down, you can also change your call settings.
- Find the Phone app and open it. Wi-Fi calling, Settings, and More (three vertical dots) are the accessible options.
- You have to tap Roaming network preference or When Roaming on certain providers. When the Wi-Fi Calling capability is enabled, the following options are available:
    - Calls will be made through your cellular network if possible. If the cellphone network is down,
    - Wi-Fi is preferred: Calls will be made via your phone's Wi-Fi network. If Wi-Fi is not accessible, the cellular network will be utilized.

Having issues with Wi-Fi Calling

When you are unable to make or receive Wi-Fi calls, there are a few things you can do to troubleshoot your phone. For Wi-Fi calling to function, you need to be linked to a Wi-Fi network. You will want a strong internet connection to make use of this feature. Check the Wi-Fi icon to determine whether you're connected to a Wi-Fi network before swiping down with two fingers to access the Quick Settings menu. You need to install your SIM card and update your address in case of an emergency before you can use Wi-Fi Calling. You can also check whether the feature is compatible with your phone's OS. If none of these solutions work, you should get in touch with your service provider.

How to activate or disable mobile data?

Mobile data refers to the internet connection provided by a mobile network carrier. Simply turning it on or off or setting it to automatically connect to a Wi-Fi network when one becomes available are all you need to do to save mobile data. Read on for details on how to toggle mobile data on and off. Be sure you're using the most current version of your device's software and any related apps before trying any of the solutions provided below. **To install software updates on your mobile device, follow these steps:**

1. Select **Software Update** from the **Settings** menu to update your software.
2. From the drop-down option, choose **Download and Install**.
3. Just follow the on-screen instructions.
4. You can turn on or off Mobile data from that point on.

If you have a SIM card and a mobile data plan, mobile data will be enabled by default. Read on for instructions on how to disable or enable mobile data.

1. After you start the Settings app, choose Connections.
2. Press Use of data.

3.   Be careful to enable mobile data. To disable mobile data, just tap the switch.

Another option is to utilize the Quick panel to toggle Mobile data on and off. Once you've uncovered the Quick panel by swiping down from the top of the screen, hit the Mobile data icon to activate or disable this feature. Keep in mind that there can be additional charges for mobile data services. To find out how much data is available to you, it's wise to contact your network provider.

How can I turn on Data Saver?

By decreasing the amount of background data consumed by programs, data saver helps you preserve data. Read on for details on how to turn on Data Saver.

1.   Go to the **Settings app** and go to the **Connections** option.
2.   Choose an option for data use.
3.   From the option that appears, choose **Data Saver**.
4.   Choose the option that says **"Turn on now"** to turn on Data Saver.

You can also choose which apps will keep using your mobile data even when Data Saver is on. When the data saver is turned on, choose the apps you want to allow access to by tapping the corresponding button. You can also access these options by navigating to **Settings** > **Apps** > **Select the app** > **Mobile data** > **Allow app** while Data saver is on. Keep in mind that the menus and images could look different on different devices and software versions.

Switching on Mobile Hotspot

Users can let other phones join and utilize their network using the mobile hotspot feature. When you activate Mobile Hotspot, all other Wi-Fi functions will be disabled as well. Turn off Data Saver if you're having trouble using Mobile Hotspot. See below for information on how to enable Hotspot.

1.   Slide up from the center of the screen on a Home screen to access the apps screen.
2.   Select **Mobile Hotspot and Tethering** from the **Connections** menu in **Settings**.
3.   Choose Mobile Hotspot.
4.   Press and hold the On button to activate or deactivate the Mobile Hotspot feature.
5.   If prompted, review the information, and then click OK to confirm.

Just like connecting to your home Wi-Fi, after you've enabled Mobile Hotspot on your Samsung Galaxy S24, you can connect any device that's compatible with your Hotspot name.

•   On your second device, find the Wi-Fi networks that are available. Select the name of the Galaxy S24 hotspot. Then, follow the onscreen steps to join and connect to the network.

- You should check the reliability of your phone's wireless internet connection. Verify that your mobile device is also completely charged. Mobile hotspots and Bluetooth tethering are two examples of wireless services that can quickly drain your phone's battery life.

Changing the Mobile Hotspot Settings

To prevent unauthorized devices from connecting to your S24 Mobile Hotspot, follow these detailed instructions to change the default password.

1. Slide up from the center of the screen on a Home screen to access the apps screen. Default Home screen layout and Standard mode are the only aspects addressed by these instructions.
2. You can access **mobile hotspot and tethering** in the **Settings app** by opening the **Connections** menu.
3. Choose Mobile Hotspot.
4. Go to the menu and choose Configure.
5. In the Password field, type in the password you'd want to use. The minimum length for a password is eight characters.
6. Select "Save" from the menu. Keep in mind that the linked device will be the one to enter the new password.

NFC and Payment

How to use NFC payment to pay

1. **Access Settings:** Find the Settings app on your smartphone.
2. **Go to Contactless Payment Settings:** Find the option for contactless payments in the Settings app and tap on it. Something along the lines of "Contactless Payment" can describe this.
3. **Verify NFC Settings:** Verify that the "NFC and Contactless Payments" toggle is in the "On" position located in the upper right corner. You can't use the contactless payment features without this.
4. **Tap Contactless Payments:** Inside the contactless payment settings, you should see an option that says "Contactless Payments."
5. **Choose Default Payment Service:** To make one payment service the default for all contactless payments, choose it from the list.
6. **View Active Wallets:** You can view all of your active wallets under the "Contactless Payments" section. Everything associated with purchasing your device falls under this category.
7. **Manage Default Wallet:** If you've enabled multiple wallets, you can change the default at any moment. Make the required adjustments to the settings on the "Payment" page to establish your chosen default wallet.

CHAPTER TWENTY

HOW TO USE VPN

Virtual private networks (VPNs) provide a wide range of capabilities. On the other hand, they are also popular among individuals who wish to add an extra degree of privacy and security, especially while using public Wi-Fi. Businesses often use them as internal networks, but they are also popular among individuals.

How to set up a VPN

This can change based on the device and the requirements that you have. (In the meantime, before you begin, you are required to choose a virtual private network (VPN) service provider. There is a wide variety of virtual private network (VPN) services available. There is a significant majority of them that charge a monthly cost that varies according to the kind of service that they provide. You can search for virtual private network (VPN) services on the Play Store. To utilize the virtual private network (VPN), you can either use the software provided by your VPN provider or manually visit their VPN settings on your device. In the settings of more recent devices, direct virtual private networks (VPNs) can be installed and controlled. The information on the VPN setup will need to be provided to you by your VPN provider.

Don't forget to bear in mind:

- If you are utilizing your virtual private network (VPN) via the provider's app, you do not need to follow the instructions on this page.
- To determine whether or not your device already has a virtual private network (VPN) activated, go to **Options > Connections > More Connection Settings> VPN**. Your device will display any virtual private networks (VPNs) that have been configured in the past.

How can I apply a VPN setup to my mobile device manually?

1. **Access the Options Menu:** Open the Options menu on your device. This will allow you to access the options menu. This is represented by a gear icon, three vertical dots, or another sign, depending on the S24 device you are using.
2. **Select Connections:** Go to the Options menu and select the "Connections" option from the list of categories.
3. **Navigate to VPN Settings:** Depending on the operating system of your device, you may be required to pick "More connection options" or "More networks."
4. **Access VPN Settings:** To access the VPN settings, go to the Connections or More Networks area and pick the "VPN" option from the list of available options.

Kindly take note that on some devices, you can see a "+" sign rather than the More symbol, which is represented by three vertical dots. In such a scenario, you should continue by selecting the "+" sign.

5. **Initiate VPN Profile Addition:** Begin the process of adding a VPN profile by selecting the "Add VPN profile" option to begin the process of setting a new VPN connection.
6. **Enter VPN Information:** The next step is to enter the essential information for your virtual private network (VPN). This information can include the server address, the kind of VPN, the username, the password, and any other data that are needed.
7. **Save VPN Profile:** Once you have entered the VPN information, choose the "Save" option to permanently preserve the newly created VPN profile on your device.

It is important to note that your VPN service provider will provide you with the particular information that is necessary for the setting of your VPN.

Protect your Private Web Browsing With a Password

Although nothing on the internet can be considered anonymous, private browsing settings can assist in concealing your activities from anybody who could have access to your data. This is true regardless of the web browser that you use. The **"secret mode"** feature of the Samsung Internet app for Android takes things to the next level by encrypting your private browsing activity with a password that is only accessible once. All individuals have their motives for using secret mode, which is sometimes referred to as **private or incognito mode**. However, there are several situations in which we do not want our personal browser history to be disclosed. Establishing a password for the secret mode is a simple method that can be used to ensure that the information that you may desire to retain is confidential.

Enabling a Password for Secret Mode

The process of generating a password for secret mode is not difficult at all.

- Hit the vertical ellipsis in the top-right corner of the screen to begin, then choose **"Settings,"** then **"Privacy,"** and finally **"Secret mode security."** This will give you access to the menu.
- By tapping the slider that is located next to the phrase **"Use password"** in the Secret mode security section, you will be able to access a password generation tool. It is important to note that Samsung Internet requires that your password be at least four characters long and include at least one letter. Although it is admirable that they are advocating a "safer" password, security cannot be achieved with just four characters. If you want to prevent anyone from the outside from using your secret mode browser, you will need to develop something more robust.

- After entering your password, you will need to confirm it by clicking the **"Continue"** button. If you hit "Continue" once again, Samsung Internet will redirect you to the security page for the Secret mode interface.

Using Biometrics

You have the option of unlocking secret mode on Samsung smartphones like the S24 Series by utilizing biometric passkeys like your fingerprint or iris scan. There are also other options available. To enter a secret mode session, you will need to check the **"Also utilize biometrics"** button while you are generating your password. This will allow you to use either your fingerprint, an iris scan, or both of these methods.

Secret Mode Browsing

Go to the bottom-right corner of the screen and tap the "Tabs" button to see all of the tabs that are currently open. This will allow you to enter the hidden mode. Following that, you will need to hit the **"Turn On Secret Mode"** button, which will show a window that displays the secret mode if you do not have a password. However, a popup will open before you, requesting that you provide your newly established password (or biometrics). To begin a session in secret mode on a Samsung smartphone, you have the option of using your password rather than biometrics by tapping the **"Use Password"** button. After you have entered your password correctly, users can browse the web in secret mode to their heart's content, secure in the knowledge that nothing they do will be seen by anybody who has physical access to their device. It is important to note that taking screenshots is not possible while accessing the secret mode. To capture a screenshot of whatever you view on the internet, you will first need to escape the secret mode on your device.

If You Forget Your Password, What Should You Do?

You must have experienced a loss of your password... At times like these, especially when the circumstances are challenging, it happens to the best of us. There is a simple solution available if you forget your password. Unfortunately, it is necessary to delete all of the data and settings associated with the hidden mode. Keeping your password close to hand or in a password manager is the best way to ensure that you do not lose access to the hidden method of browsing.

- To reset both your password and secret mode, you will need to go back to the secret mode security page in the settings menu (**Settings –> Privacy –> Secret mode security**).
- When the box appears, press "**Reset Secret mode**," and then hit **"Reset."**
- After that, you will be allowed to return to the Secret mode security page, where the "**Use password"** option will be deleted.

Using Private DNS

When using a Samsung device, it is possible to make use of an alternative DNS server to improve surfing speed and/or security. This can be accomplished by selecting Off, Automatic, or Provider from the settings menu.

- Go to Settings
- Go to Connections
- Go to More Connection settings
- Go to Private DNS
- Go to Automatic or Private DNS provider hostname
- Put in the Corresponding data and press Save

How to control vibrations and sound

When you get a text message, email, phone call, or system alert on your Galaxy phone, you may be updated in several different ways. You can modify these notification settings to have your phone vibrate, make a sound, or inform you via a Bluetooth audio device whenever you get a notice. Access to more sophisticated sound options, such as Dolby Atmos, is also available on your mobile device.

- **Sound mode**: Change the sound mode of your smartphone without having to use the Volume buttons. This feature helps you save time. To find it, swipe down from the top of the screen to reveal the Quick settings panel, and then hit the Settings button. This will allow you to access the Quick Settings panel. Clicking on Sounds and Vibration will allow you to choose a mode. There is the choice to either Mute, Vibrate, or Sound.

Note: It is important to note that the sound mode choice, rather than the Volume keys, should be used to adjust the sound mode without compromising the levels of your unique sound.

- **Vibrations**: Alter how your smartphone vibrates as well as the frequency with which it vibrates. To find it, swipe down from the top of the screen to reveal the Quick settings panel, and then hit the Settings button. This will allow you to access the Quick Settings panel. Choose Vibrate from the option that is located under Sounds and Vibration. Following that, make adjustments to the options for the Call vibration pattern, the Notification vibration pattern, and the Vibration intensity.
- **Volume**: The level of ringtones for phone calls, notifications, media, and system sounds can be controlled by the volume setting on the device. To find it, swipe down from the top of the screen to reveal the Quick settings panel, and then hit the Settings button. This will allow you to access the Quick Settings panel. Subsequently, choose Sounds & Vibrations, and then proceed to select Volume. Next, adjust the sliders appropriately for each kind of sound. The volume can also be controlled by using the Volume keys on your keyboard. When the button is pressed, a pop-up menu opens, which displays the current

music genre as well as the volume level. You have the option of expanding the menu by pressing it and then dragging the sliders to adjust the volume of the other possible sound types.

- **Ringtone**: You can customize the ringtone that plays when you get a call by choosing from a library of pre-programmed sounds or programming your own. To find it, swipe down from the top of the screen to choose the Quick settings panel, and then hit the Settings button. This will bring up the Quick Settings panel. Following that, choose Ringtone, followed by Sounds and Vibration. To use an audio file as a ringtone, you can either hit the plus symbol (+) or touch a ringtone to listen to a preview of it and then choose it.

- **Sound for notification alerts**: Choose a sound to be used for all notification updates by using the "Sound for notification alerts" option. To find it, swipe down from the top of the screen to reveal the Quick settings panel, and then hit the Settings button. This will allow you to access the Quick Settings panel. Tap the Notification sound option, followed by the Sounds and Vibration option. Tap a sound and then choose it to hear a trial version of the sound.

It is important to take note that the App settings area gives you the ability to create unique notification sounds for each app.

- **System sound**: Select a sound theme for touch interactions, charging, modifying the sound mode, and using the Samsung Keyboard, among other things, when it comes to the system sound. To find it, swipe down from the top of the screen to choose the Quick settings panel, and then hit the Settings button. This will bring up the Quick Settings panel. This is followed by clicking on Sounds and Vibration, followed by System Sound. Take a sound from the list and choose it.

- **Notification pop-up style**: Changing the notification pop-up style allows you to prioritize and optimize app alerts by allowing you to choose which apps send notifications and how notifications inform you individually. To find it, swipe down from the top of the screen to choose the Quick settings panel, and then hit the Settings button. This will bring up the Quick Settings panel. Make your selection from the Notifications menu for the pop-up style. You have the option of selecting between Brief or Detailed alerts, and then you can tailor the notifications according to your preferences.

- **Recently sent notifications**: Notifications that have been issued lately will allow you to browse through a list of programs that have recently provided alerts. To find it, swipe down from the top of the screen to choose the Quick settings panel, and then hit the Settings button. This will bring up the Quick Settings panel. You can choose the option you wish to use under Recently sent by pressing the Notifications button. In addition, you can expand the list by pressing the More button. If necessary, you can make adjustments to the notification settings from this location.

- **Alert when phone picked up**: When you pick up your phone, the device should vibrate to alert you to any missed calls or messages. You can configure this feature to occur when you pick up your phone. To find it, swipe down from the top of the screen to choose the

Quick settings panel, and then hit the Settings button. This will bring up the Quick Settings panel. Next, choose Advanced Features, and then select Motions and Gestures from the menu. When the phone is picked up, turn on the switch that is located next to the word "Alert when the phone is picked up."

- **Equalizer:** Select from a wide range of audio presets that are specifically designed for a variety of musical styles, or you can manually adjust the parameters for your audio. Entering the Quick Settings panel by sliding downwards from the top of the screen and then selecting the Settings button will allow you to find information about it. Next, choose Sounds and Vibration, and then select Sound Quality and Effects from the menu. Tap Equalizer to choose a musical genre to listen to.

- **UHQ upscaler**: Through the use of the UHQ upscaler, the sound quality of movies and music can be enhanced, resulting in a more immersive listening experience. Entering the Quick Settings panel by sliding downwards from the top of the screen and then selecting the Settings button will allow you to find information about it. Next, choose Sounds and Vibration, and then select Sound Quality and Effects from the menu. The Upscaling option can be selected by selecting the UHQ Upscaler button.

It is important to note that the Galaxy Buds variants do not include this enabling feature. Corded headsets and Bluetooth-enabled devices are the only ones that are compatible with this product.

- **Adapt sound**: Enhance your listening experience by tailoring the sound to each ear individually. To find it, swipe down from the top of the screen to choose the Quick settings panel, and then hit the Settings button. This will bring up the Quick Settings panel. Next, choose Sounds and Vibration, and then select Sound Quality and Effects from the menu. By touching the Adapt sound button, you can choose when the sound settings will be adjusted, and then you can select the sound profile that is most suitable for you. Then, to make changes to it, hit the button marked Settings.

Make sure to click the Test My Hearing button so that your device can determine the sound that is most suitable for you.

- **Separate app sound**: You can have an application play media sounds on a Bluetooth speaker or headphones that are not mixed in with the other noises (like alerts). This allows you to have a more enjoyable experience. Entering the Quick Settings panel by sliding downwards from the top of the screen and then selecting the Settings button will allow you to find information about it. Finally, choose Sounds and Vibration, and then select Separate app sound from the menu. Tap the Turn on Now button, and then choose the appropriate settings for the App and Audio device. This will enable the Separate app sound.

Having a Bluetooth device connected is required to make use of the available audio choices.

- **Do not disturb**: This mode allows you to silence notifications and sounds when it is activated, and it is referred to as "do not disturb." In addition to this, you can make exceptions for certain people, apps, and alarms, as well as schedule routine activities like going to sleep or attending meetings. Entering the Quick Settings panel by sliding downwards from the top of the screen and then selecting the Settings button will allow you to find information about it. The Notifications and Do Not Disturb settings can be toggled between. You can configure several different settings, including Do Not Disturb, for how long, Sleeping, Add schedule, Calls, messages, and chats, Alarms and sounds, Apps, and Hide notifications.
- **Advanced settings**: Customize app and service notifications via the advanced settings in the app. You can find it by swiping down from the top of the screen to open the Quick Settings window and then clicking the Settings button upon entering the window. Next, choose Notifications, and then select Advanced Settings from the menu. Show notification icons, Show battery %, Notification history, Conversations, Floating notifications, Suggest actions and answers for notifications, Notification reminders, Application icon badges, and Wireless Emergency Alerts are just a few of the options available.

CHAPTER TWENTY-ONE
TROUBLESHOOTING COMMON ISSUES

Wi-Fi stops working?

If you have problems with the performance of your Wi-Fi on your Galaxy S24 smartphone, particularly when you are unable to connect to a network after making several efforts, you should take into consideration the following troubleshooting procedures to resolve the issue:

- **Starting with the fundamentals:** Before anything else, you should investigate the core components of your Wi-Fi configuration. Confirm that your Wi-Fi is switched on; while it can seem to be a simple task, you may have missed the opportunity to enable the Wi-Fi function or been unable to click the button completely. Make sure that the Wi-Fi button on your smartphone has been engaged correctly by clicking on it many times to check the state of the button.
- **Disable Bluetooth:** Bluetooth interference might be a possible reason that affects Wi-Fi access. While both technologies often operate inside the 2.4GHz frequency range, Bluetooth interference can be especially problematic. Because of the frequency that is shared, interference may occur. To avoid this issue, you should deactivate Bluetooth on your device anytime you have problems with your Wi-Fi connection. Additionally, the general performance of your Wi-Fi connection will be improved as a result of this procedure, which helps prevent any conflicts.

Samsung Galaxy S24 Series Network Issues

You can cause this network problem with almost any Android smartphone. If your Samsung phone has poor signal strength or an unreliable mobile network.

Think about these guidelines:

Solutions

- Verify whether a software update is necessary for your device. Update it if it is available.
- Please power down your device. Take the SIM card out of your Samsung Galaxy S24 and put it back.
- Open the notification panel. Activate airplane mode for a few seconds then turn it off.
- To return the network settings to their factory defaults, go to **SIM & Network Access Point Names**.
- Possible network issues after unlocking the bootloader, installing a custom ROM, or performing a recovery.
- Go into the Network settings and make sure that Roaming services are turned on.
- If you think the problem could be on your end, you should contact your network provider.

- Restart your Samsung Galaxy S24 Series device after you have finished the preceding instructions.

Lagging on the Samsung Galaxy S24 Series

Is the UI on your smartphone slow and unresponsive? Here is how to repair your smartphone if that's the case. This problem with smartphones affects almost everyone, and it is now the most pervasive problem with all gadgets combined. Even with brand-new phones, this might happen since we tend to fill up RAM on newer models with apps and data that we no longer need. To avoid any confusion, read the following solution carefully.

Solutions

- See whether your Samsung Galaxy S24 Series phone is becoming too hot. The device has overheated and stopped functioning in several ways.
- How many tabs have you opened in your browser? Put an end to it if that's so. The more tabs you have open, the more RAM your phone will need.
- For the device to work properly, your phone's internal storage capacity must be sufficient.
- Clean up your smartphone by removing any unnecessary applications, like antivirus and trash cleaners.
- Is latency something you've encountered after installing an app recently? In such instances, uninstall the software that is responsible for the problem.
- Class 10 microSD cards are faster than regular cards, so use them if your phone supports them.
- Get the latest software version for your phone if it's available.
- Is there not enough room in your storage unit? In such cases, you should use the lite versions of applications like Facebook, Messenger, Twitter, YouTube Go, and so on.
- Get the latest versions of all your apps from the Play Store if they have any accessible updates.
- Do you have a third-party launcher installed? Take it off immediately. The majority of the time, using several launcher programs causes the smartphone to be slow.
- You should remove any icons or font packs that were put on your phone by third parties.
- The issue should go away when you clear the cache and trash files on your device.
- There is likely a hardware problem with your Samsung Galaxy S24 Series if latency is still an issue.

The Samsung Galaxy S24 Series Bluetooth isn't functioning

Problems with Bluetooth connection and pairing can be rather annoying. Sometimes, when you try to pair your phone with your car's speakers, you can receive an error message or your phone might just not connect at all. No need to worry. What follows is a list of possible solutions to the issue.

Solutions

- Establish a Bluetooth connection in a stable setting.
- Never leave your phone in a bag or a small place.
- Make that the Bluetooth device is correctly linked to your Samsung Galaxy S24 Ultra. Incorrect matching is a common source of the problem.
- Verify that your device's Bluetooth visibility is disabled.
- Can you send a lot of files via Bluetooth at once? In particular, remember that Bluetooth can only transfer very few files and not very big ones.
- When not in use, turn off power-saving and safe modes.
- To try connecting Bluetooth again, reboot your phone.
- When Bluetooth devices are too far apart, a limited connection could happen.
- Verify whether a software update is necessary for your device. Revise it if you have the time.
- Has the problem with the Bluetooth connection persisted? Then you may want to think about wiping your Samsung Galaxy S24 Series clean.

Apps and games keep crashing

If your Samsung Galaxy S24 Series crashes whenever you try to open an app or game, don't freak out. If you follow the steps below, you should be able to fix this common problem.

Solutions

- The apps and games you're using are probably outdated. Make sure you're using the latest and current versions of all your software.
- If an application is crashing for you, try clearing its cache.
- Navigate to the following menu: **Apps > Settings > Three dots > Reset App Preferences**. Make sure you ask about the status of the issue's resolution.
- A virus on your phone might be the culprit.
- Check whether there is a new software version available for the Samsung Galaxy S24 Series. Revise it if you have the time.
- Try restarting your phone to resolve the problem.
- Make sure to disable power saving mode on your Samsung Galaxy S24 Series if it is enabled.

Samsung Galaxy S24 Series camera difficulties

Do you find that the camera quality on your Samsung Galaxy S24 Series is lacking? In such instances, these methods have been effective in the past, and they will help you fix the issue.

Solutions

- A bug in the Android OS is to blame for this issue. You will have to be patient until your device's maker releases an official update before it will be fixed.
- Has the installation of a third-party camera app caused you to encounter this issue? Delete it and install the official camera app if that's the case.
- If you want your camera to take the greatest shots, use the image stabilization feature.
- Remove any data stored by the camera app by opening it. Before you proceed, be sure this fixes the problem.
- The camera app has an HD option that you should choose.
- If your phone comes with a glass screen protector already installed, take it off.
- If the photographs are becoming too dark, use the flashlight that is included with your camera.
- You can see this problem if you adjust the camera's settings. Try resetting the camera to factory settings to see if that helps.
- Disable any filters that may be affecting your phone's camera.
- Try cleaning the lens of your Samsung Galaxy S24 Ultra and seeing if it helps.
- The Samsung Galaxy S24 Ultra's camera is malfunctioning due to a hardware problem.

Samsung Galaxy S24 Series battery drains quickly

Almost every person who uses a smartphone has experienced this problem. If you're experiencing a problem with your Samsung Galaxy S24 series battery draining quickly, try the solutions provided below.

Solutions

- Remove RAM booster applications and other garbage-cleaning software. These apps constantly use power as they operate in the background.
- Disable auto-brightness and lower the brightness while it's not in use.
- To set the minimum screen timeout to 30 seconds, go to **Settings > Display > Screen timeout > Minimum Screen timeout**. The screen will turn off automatically while your phone is not being used.
- To activate power saving mode on your Samsung Galaxy S24 Ultra, access the power saving mode menu that appears in the notification area.
- Remember to disable location services (Bluetooth, GPS, etc.) while they are not in use.
- When you enable mobile data, you may notice that your battery life decreases.
- While your device is in Safe mode, examine whether the issue still exists.
- Turn off notifications for non-essential apps.
- Your device may have a malware infection. It could be cleaned up using antivirus software.

- If you spend a lot of time watching movies or playing games, you can end up with this problem.
- Bring your Samsung Galaxy S24 Series phone into a Samsung service center to get it checked out if the issue with the battery draining continues.

Text Messages Cannot Be Sent or Received on the Samsung Galaxy S24 Series

Solutions

- Make sure you have sufficient SMS credit on your phone before trying to send a text.
- Remove any unnecessary communications and see whether the issue persists.
- Remove all data and cache from the messaging app for the Samsung Galaxy S24 Series. Compose a message immediately.
- It's possible that restarting your phone can fix the problem.
- To test whether the problem persists after turning off the Airplane/Flight mode, try turning it on again.
- Verify the recipient's status in the contact app to ensure they are not on the prohibited list.
- To determine whether the issue is with your network provider, you should contact them.

The Samsung Galaxy S24 Series has been stuck on the boot screen

Does the "Samsung" logo keep popping up on your Samsung Galaxy S24 Series, making it fail to boot up? If that's the case, you shouldn't worry. Perhaps we can lend you a hand in fixing this issue so it's operational again soon. Below you will find a list of possible remedies to the frustrating boot loop or soft brick problem.

Solutions

To restart the Samsung Galaxy S24 Series, press and hold the Power button and the Volume Down button at the same time. This will cause the device to reset. In most cases, this will clear the memory and get the gadget going again.

Enter Safe Mode on the Samsung Galaxy S24 Series:

1. If you are unable to power down your phone in any other way, then turn it off. Please wait until the battery is completely dead before powering down the phone.
2. Maintain a steady press on the Power key. When you see the Samsung logo, press the Volume Down key right away.

3. After the phone has rebooted into safe mode, identify the problem. The boot loop is probably being generated by a program.
4. Revert to your phone's normal setting by removing the app.
5. If the problem persists, try again with steps 1-4.
   - On Samsung Galaxy S24 models, you can access recovery mode by: After booting into recovery mode, clear the cache partition as a first step. Resetting your phone to factory settings can help if that doesn't work.
   - Contact the Samsung Service Center to get your phone repaired if the issue continues after you've followed the aforementioned steps.

The Samsung Galaxy S24 Series is unable to connect to WiFi

Does your Samsung Galaxy S24 Series fail to connect to WiFi networks even after providing the correct password? In such an instance, fix your Samsung phone's WiFi problem by following the steps provided below.

Solutions

Disconnect from Wifi and Reconnect:

1. Make sure to open the wifi settings.
2. Toggle between the Wifi network and Forget.
3. After that, toggle the WiFi on and off on the Samsung Galaxy S24 Series.
4. Next, join the wireless network by touching it, then enter the password, and finally reconnect.
5. Find out how many gadgets are connected to the WiFi. If the network's device count is too high, this issue could arise.
6. Get the network settings of your device reset: Press the Reset buttons next to Wifi, Mobile, and Bluetooth in the Settings menu to do this.
7. Try power cycling your wireless network and phone as a last resort. Without a doubt, this will resolve the problem.

Samsung Galaxy S24 Ultra Overheating Issues

If your phone is often becoming hot, there are a few possible causes for it, including the battery or another issue. It is common for your phone to become heated when you are using it.

This is often a sign of high-intensity processing tasks performed at work, such as multitasking, gaming, or streaming music.

The steps listed below will help you solve the heating issue.

Solutions

- Try closing any background apps to see if it resolves the problem.
- Check to see if a simple restart fixes the problem with your Samsung phone.
- Switch off Bluetooth, GPS, Wi-Fi, and other connectivity options while not in use.
- Disable the auto-brightness function from the notification panel.
- Could this issue have been caused by charging your phone with a power bank? It is the main reason if that is the case.
- If you play games on your smartphone while it's charging, it might overheat.
- The temperature outside might be to blame for the device's overheating.
- To check if it helps, try rebooting your Samsung Galaxy S24 Series phone in safe mode.
- Verify that the applications and software on your phone are up to date.
- You may have a heating issue with your phone if it has a lot of applications installed.
- Remove any games or programs that are not being used.
- The maximum amount of internal storage should be made available. There's little question that this will improve your phone's overall performance.
- You should anticipate some warming if you play games with high-end graphics.
- Scan your phone with antivirus software on your PC. A virus on your phone is probably the source of the heating issue.

App not installed problem

If you try to install an app from a .apk file and get an **"app not installed"** warning, don't worry. This is a very common issue. Use the steps listed below to fix the Samsung Galaxy S24 Series app not installed issue.

Solutions

- There's a chance the apk file you're trying to install is damaged. Once again, attempt to obtain the file from a reliable source.
- Maybe the software you downloaded isn't compatible with your device. Put in an earlier version of the program. This will resolve the problem.
- Verify that Install from Unknown Sources is turned on for your Samsung Galaxy S24 Series device before installing any program files.

Look below:

1. Open the Settings menu and choose Security.
2. Make Unknown Sources Active.
3. Reinstall the application.

Disable Google Play Protect by following these steps

1. Open the Google Play store first.
2. Choose Menu Play Protect Settings by clicking on the drop-down option.
3. The option to "Scan applications with Play Protect" has been disabled.
4. Next, try to reinstall the software.

Samsung Galaxy S24 Series App Preferences Reset

1. Access the settings on your phone.
2. In the Apps & Notifications section, tap on Apps.
3. Finally, hit the three dots, then choose Reset app settings.

NOTE: One of the most common reasons why an application won't install is insufficient storage. Clear some space on your hard disk and attempt to download the software once again.

Randomly, the Samsung Galaxy S24 Series goes off

If the random discharge of your Samsung Galaxy S24 Ultra smartphone continues occurring, there may be a hardware or software issue. **You can easily fix this problem by following the guidelines shown below:**

Solutions

- Verify that the temperature of your phone isn't too high; this might be the reason for the unplanned shutdown.
- Steer clear of bulky phone cases. This might lead to improper heat ventilation, which would cause your phone to shut off.
- To check whether an app is the source of the issue, start the Samsung Galaxy S24 Series in Safe Mode.
- Scan your device with a PC anti-virus program.
- Try the aforementioned procedures and hard reset your Samsung Galaxy S24 Series if the issue still doesn't go away.

You can't make or receive phone calls

When calling someone and receiving the message "Can't Make or Receive Calls," network problems are often to blame. Use the steps listed below to resolve the Samsung Galaxy S24 Series issue of not being able to make or receive phone calls.

Solutions

- Take the SIM card out of your phone and put it back in after ten seconds.
- Verify whether the Airplane mode was inadvertently activated. Verify that it is off.

- Return to the original configuration by going to Network Settings. Verify if the problem has been fixed.
- Give your gadget a single restart. See what happens when you give it a try.
- It's conceivable that you are trying to contact a blocked phone number. If the contact is on the block list, remove it.
- One common reason for this problem is that the network selection mode is set to manual mode. Try setting it to Automatic to see if it fixes the problem.
- If it is available, update the software on your phone to the most current version.
- Verify that you have sufficient credit on your phone before making a call.

Apps not downloading from the Play Store

The Google Play Store isn't letting you download the software you want to, it says "download pending." It's past time to deal with the issue. Use the steps listed below to fix the Samsung Galaxy S24 Series phone's app not downloading issue.

Solutions

- Verify whether you're trying to install a program when another is updating. You have two options: wait for the program to be updated before downloading it, or abort the download.
- Clear the Google Play Store's cache and data.
- Additionally, delete all of the data and cache for the Download Manager and Play Services applications.
- Select **Over any network** in the Play Store by tapping on the **app download preference** under **Settings** > **Network Preferences**.
- Reinstall the Play Store updates after uninstalling them.
- Verify that your phone has enough space on it before installing the app.
- Try giving your phone a quick restart to see if it fixes the problem.

The microphone isn't functioning

When you're on the phone, is the caller unable to hear you or are you trying to record your voice? If so, rectify the issue by following the steps listed below.

Solutions

- Try starting your phone in Safe Mode again and see whether the microphone works as it should. If it works, a third-party app on your smartphone is the source of the problem.
- Determine if any software upgrades are still due. Install it after downloading it if it's accessible.
- Delete the data and cache for the voice recording app.
- If the person you're speaking with is unable to hear you, there may be a network problem.

- Try restarting your device to see if it resolves the problem.
- Reset the factory settings on your Samsung Galaxy S24 Series device. Without a doubt, this will fix the microphone problem.
- Visit the manufacturer's service center to get your equipment fixed if the issue continues.

Unlock isn't functioning

If you attempt to use face unlock on your Samsung Galaxy S24 Series device and it fails, don't lose hope. It is a minor issue that can be fixed with a few adjustments.

Solutions

- Give your phone a restart and see if that helps.
- You can switch the Samsung Galaxy S24 Series face lock on and off.
- Reapply your face after erasing any previous facial data.
- Verify that the sensor on your front camera is clean. Dirt may have gathered on your phone's camera sensor, making it unable to recognize your face.
- Verify that nothing is blocking the selfie camera.
- Take off any headgear, sunglasses, or masks you may be wearing to test whether your smartphone unlocks.
- Verify that the operating system on your phone is current.
- To check whether the face unlock issue has been fixed, hard reset the Samsung Galaxy S24 Series.

CHAPTER TWENTY-TWO
ADVANCED TIPS AND TRICKS
LIVE TRANSLATE DURING CALLS

Have you ever been on the phone with someone who doesn't speak the same language as you? If you don't understand the other person completely, things might turn awkward and nasty. Fortunately, you can use the Live Translate feature of the Galaxy S24 Ultra while on the phone. When you turn this on, the phone will translate your phrases into the recipient's language while you talk in your tongue. Their phrases will also be translated into your tongue of origin in actual time. Sounds good, doesn't it? This is how you activate it.

Step 1: Tap the three dots in the upper right corner of the Phone app after opening it. Choose Settings from this menu.

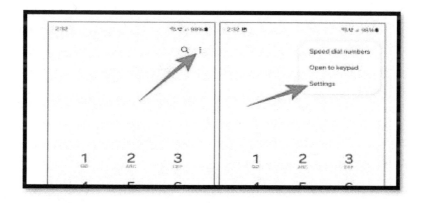

Step 2: Navigate to the Call Assist area inside the Call settings page. Click **"Live translate"** there. Next, turn on the Live Translate toggle.

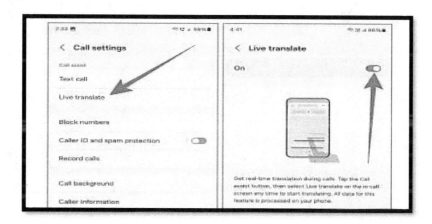

Step 3: You can set the language preferences for each party below it. You can even customize the voice that the system uses to talk for you when it speaks. An additional option is to "Mute my voice." If you turn this on, the other person will only hear the translated version and your voice won't be muted when you're on a call utilizing this option.

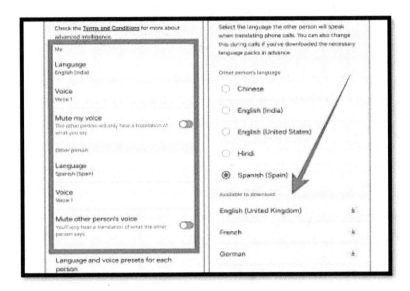

Step 4: After it has been activated, you will be able to make use of this function while you are on a call. To do this, choose the 'Call Assist' option while you are currently on a call. Then, choose the 'Live translate' option. Exactly, that is it. Following the settings that you have specified, your Galaxy S24 Ultra will immediately begin translating the voices of both parties simultaneously.

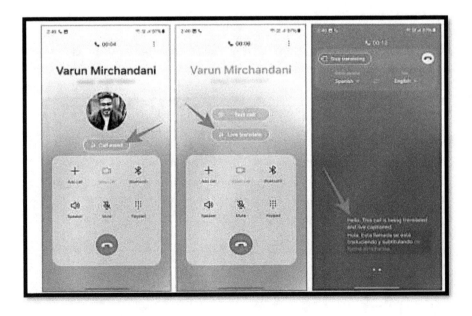

INTERPRETER MODE

However, despite how effective Live Translate is, it is only useful for phone conversations. Consider the following scenario: you are in a foreign nation, you are attempting to bargain with the proprietor of a store, and you want a translation. You can indeed use Google Translate, but the Galaxy S24 Ultra takes one step further by providing a mode that is specifically designed to interpret. As they talk, their voice is translated and transcribed right on the phone, and it is shown straightforwardly so that both of you can easily comprehend and reply to what is being presented. The greatest thing is that you can accomplish all of this on your phone, without the requirement for any kind of internet connection or a single access point to the internet. This is how you should utilize it.

Step 1: Navigate to the main menu and choose Settings > Advanced features > Advanced intelligence. After that, choose the Interpreter option.

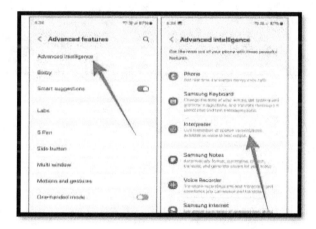

Step 2: The second step is to choose the "Language packs for translation" option. After that, you will be able to download the languages that you need for translation.

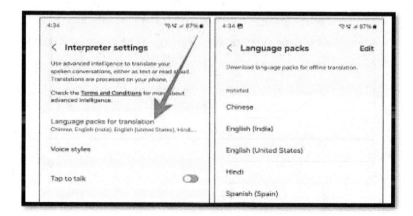

Step 3: The third step is to slide down the notification tray after you have finished, which will display the quick settings toggles. Tap on the Interpreter button here.

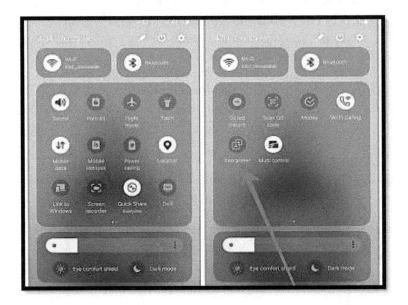

Step 4: The Interpreter app should now be open, which is the fourth step. To initiate the translation process, you just tap on any of the microphone symbols. Exactly, that is it. When you speak into the Galaxy S24 Ultra, your voice will be translated into the language that you have chosen almost instantly. After that, it will automatically listen for the other person to talk and then translate what they say back into your language.

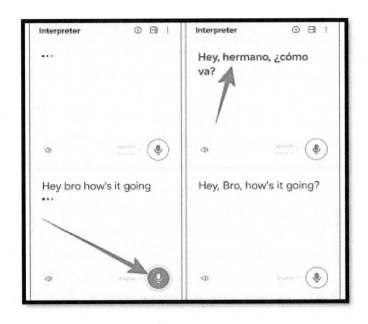

SUMMARIZE NOTES

Because it has a large number of capabilities, the Notes app that comes pre-installed on the Galaxy S24 is considered to be among the greatest note-taking applications currently available. Because of this, the length of your notes may become extremely extensive. You can utilize artificial intelligence to reduce your extensive notes into summaries, which is one of the greatest tips and tricks for the Galaxy S24 Ultra. In essence, it draws attention to the most important aspects, saving you valuable time. This is how you should utilize it.

Step 1: First, launch the Samsung Notes application, and then choose the stored note that you want to write a summary for. Make sure to choose the Generative AI option located in the bottom bar, as seen in the image. Click the OK button that appears in the dialog box that appears and asks for permission.

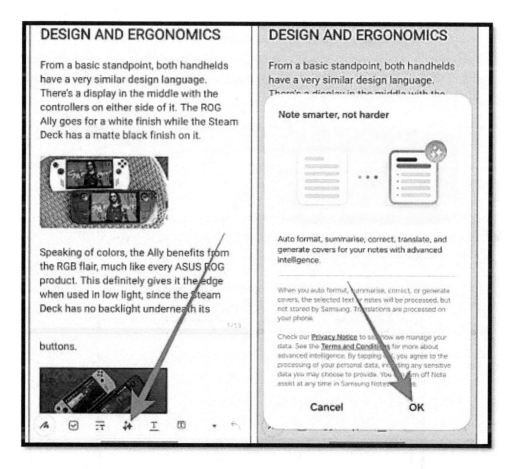

Step 2: At this point, choose the passage that you want to summarize. Select the Summarize option after you are finished. Exactly, that is it.

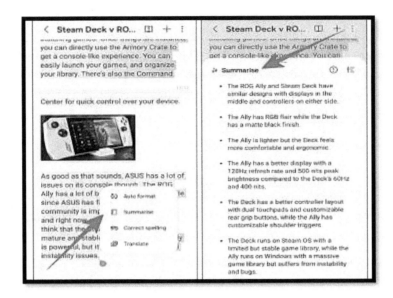

After beginning to analyze the content, the Notes app will then provide you with a short version of your notes that has been summarized.

GET TEXT TRANSCRIPTS FOR VOICE RECORDINGS

The capability of the Google Pixel 8 and 8 Pro to utilize the recorder app to get a complete transcription of the recording is among the most impressive aspects of these high-end smartphones. Samsung, on the other hand, was not going to be left behind for very long. You can quickly record lectures, interviews, or brainstorming sessions using the Samsung Galaxy S24 Ultra, and then you can let the S24 Ultra transcribe them for you. That is how you should go about doing it. You can begin playing a recording that you have saved by opening the Voice Recorder app. An option to transcribe should be available to you at this point. The only thing you need to do is choose a language and then touch the Transcribe button once again.

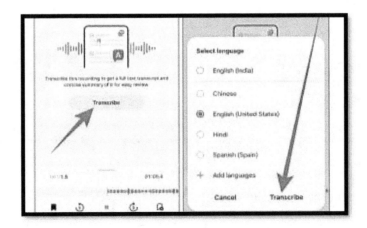

Exactly, that is it. You will first be presented with a transcript of the recording, after which the S24 Ultra will begin the processing of the recording. Additionally, if you want to get a summary of the whole recording, you can also choose the Summary option which is located at the very top of the screen.

SUMMARIZE WEB PAGES

Not only can the Galaxy S24 Ultra summarize websites in their entirety, but it can also summarize web pages in their entirety. Exactly, you are correct. By adding this artificial intelligence capability, the Samsung Internet browser, which is already considered to be one of the finest online browsers for Android, becomes even more impressive. This is how you should utilize it.

- **Step 1:** Step one is to launch the Samsung Internet Browser application and go to a website of your choice. After that, choose the Generative AI option that is located on the bottom bar. To grant it the essential permission, be sure to touch on OK.
- **Step 2:** The second step is that the application will now inquire as to whether you would want to translate the text or summarize the page. Select the Summarize option. After that, the application will need some time to analyze the data, and then it will eventually provide you with a report that summarizes the whole web page.

USE GENERATIVE EDIT

Magic Editor is just another fantastic function that is included in the Pixel range. It is interesting to note that Samsung also has an answer to this, and it comes in the shape of a Generative Edit. You can eliminate undesired items from photographs, modify the location of the subject, and perform several other functions using this capability. This is how you can put it to use.

- **Step 1:** The picture you want to modify should be opened inside the Gallery app, and then you should touch on the modify button. Select the Generative AI icon, as indicated below, and then touch on it.

- **Step 2:** In the second step, you will be able to highlight the topic that you want to change. In most circumstances, it should be sufficient to just circle it; the artificial intelligence will automatically snap to the boundaries. The selection can then be moved about, resized, or removed by pressing the erase button. Once you have finished, you can then tap and hold on to the selection to do these actions.

- **Step 3:** When you are satisfied with the modifications you have made, click the Generate button. The artificial intelligence will then fill in the blanks that are left in the picture.

- **Step 4:** To save the edited version of the picture, hit the Done button, and then press the 'Save as copy' button, respectively.

USE S-PEN AIR ACTIONS (ULTRA ONLY)

It is the S-Pen that stands out as one of the most distinctive characteristics of the Samsung Galaxy S24 Ultra. On the other hand, in addition to its function as a pen, the Pen also has support for its Air Actions. All of these functions can be performed without touching the screen, including scrolling across pages, launching applications, and switching between windows. The S-Pen icon can be accessed by opening an application that you want to interact with and then tapping on it. You should be able to see a list of all of the Air Actions that are supported by the app inside the phone. Following that, you will be able to execute those movements in the air while simultaneously hitting the Pen button, which will cause the related command to be activated.

USE CIRCLE TO SEARCH

With the Samsung Galaxy S24 Ultra, Google's Circle to Search function was also introduced on a mobile device. The name of this feature implies that users can circle, highlight, draw on, or press anything on the screen of the Galaxy S24 to get search results that are valuable and of high quality. You can learn about historical places, recognize flora, and decipher signs with the assistance of artificial intelligence. All you have to do to utilize it is press and hold the home button that is located on your navigation bar. On the other hand, if you are using Gesture Navigation, you can just press and hold the symbol that represents the navigation bar until you feel a vibration. A pop-up window for Circle to Search ought to appear at this point. Simply tap 'Try it now'.

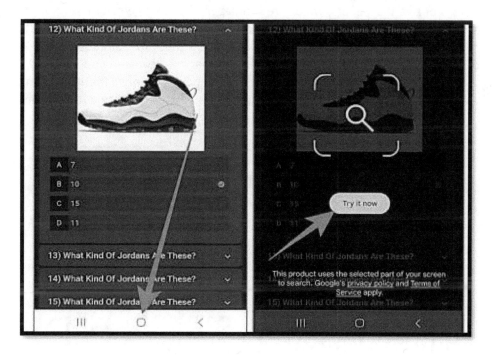

Following that, you will be able to circle the information that you want to identify or learn more about. The mobile device will automatically search for the same and provide information that is pertinent to the search.

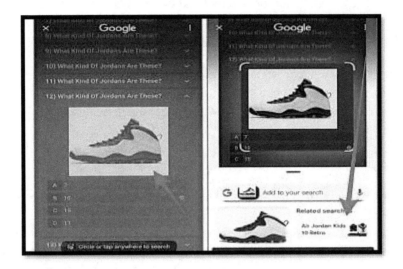

ENABLE PHOTO AMBIENT WALLPAPER

We are all fans of Live Wallpapers, which are wallpapers that change color based on the time of day, with lighter tones during the day and darker tones throughout the night. To put that into perspective, rather than using a collection of wallpapers that have already been customized, wouldn't it be wonderful if we could do that for our images? However, you can do so with the Galaxy S24 Ultra. Simply go to the **Settings** menu, then choose **Advanced features**, then **Labs**, and finally, select the 'Photo ambient wallpaper' option. Here, enable the toggle for the same.

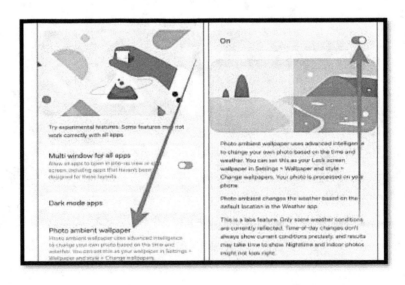

Navigate to the Settings menu, then choose Wallpaper and Style, and then select Change Wallpapers. At this point, pick the picture you want to use by tapping on the Gallery option.

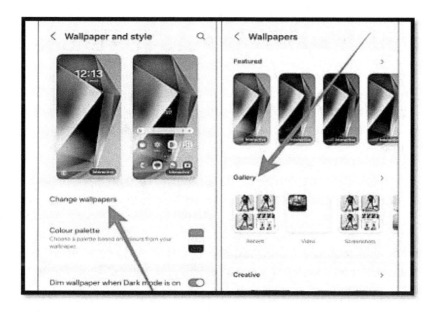

After selecting whether you want the wallpaper to be shown on the home screen, the lock screen, or both, you should then hit the Next button. If you wish to install the wallpaper, you can either edit it to your desire by adding effects, or you can just press the Done button to apply it.

Exactly, that is it. The phone will automatically adjust the picture to match the current time and weather conditions of the default location in the Weather app. This will be done based on the information provided by the Weather app.

SET DIFFERENT AUDIO OUTPUTS FOR EACH APP

The fact that you can even establish distinct audio outputs for each app on your S24 Ultra is something you probably did not know. As an example, you can play music via your headphones while still maintaining the ability to hear navigation instructions through the speakers of your phone. For this, just go to the **Settings** menu, then choose **Sounds and Vibration**, and then select **Separate app sound**.

Now, turn on the toggle that is located next to the phrase **"Turn on now." Select** should then be tappe d. Select the applications that you want to play on a different audio device as the first step. After that, hit the back button. At this point, you should be able to choose the audio device that will be used for the output. At this point, you should return to the settings page. Exactly, that is it. Those particular applications will only output to the audio device that has been allocated to them, whilst the other applications will operate with the default audio output, which is the speakers on your smartphone.

USE MODES AND ROUTINES

Along the same lines as the Galaxy S23 series, the Galaxy S24 Ultra is equipped with a function that is referred to as Modes and Routines. This enables you to do things on your smartphone in an automated fashion, eliminating the need for you to carry them out manually. You can use it to build personalized profiles that will modify the settings of your phone depending on the environment you are in or the activities you are doing. While the Sleep Mode reduces the brightness of the screen and mutes alerts, the Work Mode helps you concentrate on what you're doing by reducing the number of distractions you face.

Imagine that Modes are the helpers that are always ready to be triggered anytime you want their assistance. Routines, on the other hand, are quiet partners that automatically spring into action when certain circumstances are fulfilled. Routines are silent partners. Move to **Settings** > **Modes and Routines** > **Modes** to make use of the Modes feature. Currently, you have the choice of selecting a mode from the available options or creating a mode that is unique to your preferences. To change your routines, just choose the Routines tab located at the bottom of the screen. You can either design your Routines or search for recommended Routines by tapping on the compass symbol located at the top of the screen.

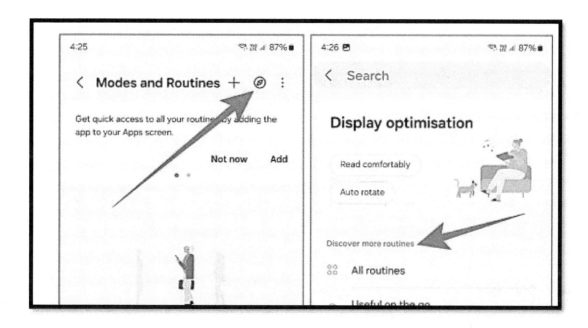

CONCLUSION

This Samsung guide is your complete companion for realizing the full potential of your Samsung devices, with a special emphasis on the Samsung Galaxy S24. Throughout the guide, we've thoroughly examined the S24's features and functions, giving step-by-step instructions, insightful suggestions, and troubleshooting answers to help you get the most out of this cutting-edge technology. The guide's well-organized layout is intended to appeal to users of all skill levels, from computer newbies to seasoned specialists. Whether you're setting up your S24 for the first time, customizing its features, or resolving any issues, our layout allows for a smooth exploration of your device's possibilities. This guide's attention to detail in resolving typical Samsung Galaxy S24 questions and issues is a standout feature. We want to improve your user experience by providing clear explanations and proactive solutions, allowing you to confidently use your S24. As you navigate the fast-changing technological world, this guide will remain a dynamic resource, updated regularly to reflect the most recent software releases and features. Our objective is to give you more than just a guidebook, but a timely and comprehensive tool that will allow you to maximize your Samsung experience.

INDEX

B

D

E

F

G

H

I

N

T

U

V

W

Y

Z

www.ingramcontent.com/pod-product-compliance
Lightning Source LLC
LaVergne TN
LVHW081521050326
832903LV00025B/1568